DIVINE
DISRUPTION

DIVINE
DISRUPTION

Holding on to Faith
When Life Breaks Your Heart

Dr. Tony Evans, Chrystal Evans Hurst,
Priscilla Shirer, Anthony Evans,
& Jonathan Evans

with Jamie Blaine

W PUBLISHING GROUP

AN IMPRINT OF THOMAS NELSON

Published in Nashville, Tennessee, by W Publishing, an imprint of Thomas Nelson.

Thomas Nelson titles may be purchased in bulk for educational, business, fundraising, or sales promotional use. For information, please e-mail SpecialMarkets@ThomasNelson.com.

Unless otherwise noted, Scripture quotations are taken from the Christian Standard Bible®, Copyright © 2017 by Holman Bible Publishers. Used by permission. Christian Standard Bible® and CSB®, are federally registered trademarks of Holman Bible Publishers.

Scripture quotations marked KJV are taken from the King James Version. Public domain.

Scripture quotations marked NCV are taken from the New Century Version®. Copyright © 2005 by Thomas Nelson. Used by permission. All rights reserved.

Scripture quotations marked NKJV are taken from the New King James Version®. Copyright © 1982 by Thomas Nelson. Used by permission. All rights reserved.

Scripture quotations marked NIV are taken from The Holy Bible, New International Version®, NIV®. Copyright © 1973, 1978, 1984, 2011 by Biblica, Inc.® Used by permission of Zondervan. All rights reserved worldwide. www.Zondervan.com. The "NIV" and "New International Version" are trademarks registered in the United States Patent and Trademark Office by Biblica, Inc.®

Scripture quotations marked NLT are taken from the Holy Bible, New Living Translation. © 1996, 2004, 2015 by Tyndale House Foundation. Used by permission of Tyndale House Publishers, Inc., Carol Stream, Illinois 60188. All rights reserved.

ISBN 978-0-7852-4117-1 (audiobook)
ISBN 978-0-7852-4116-4 (eBook)

Library of Congress Control Number: 2021943893

ISBN 978-0-7852-4114-0

Printed in the United States of America

21 22 23 24 25 LSC 10 9 8 7 6 5 4 3 2 1

If God showed us the whole journey,
we'd never take the first step.

—DR. LOIS EVANS

CONTENTS

CONTENTS

LIFE INTERRUPTED

But the fruit of the Spirit is love, joy, peace, patience, kindness,
goodness, faithfulness, gentleness, and self-control.
—GALATIANS 5:22–23

ANTHONY EVANS (JR.)

Gentle strength. That is my mother, her spirit, the way she carried herself. Mom was never aggressive. True strength does not need to push or be loud. It's quiet, calm. Gentle strength comes from the peace that passes understanding, from resting in the Lord.

Whether Sunday morning, Wednesday-night church, or gathered in the kitchen at home, Dr. Lois Evans was the same, and this is how we were raised—Chrystal, Priscilla, Jonathan, and me. With that same gentle strength, in the most difficult moments of her fight, she looked each of us straight in the eye and said, "I want you to be doing ministry together."

All four of us are involved in some form of ministry individually, each of us doing our own thing. I've been in and out of Los Angeles for years, working in the film and television industry while continuing to do gospel and worship music. Occasionally, we would work together on projects, Priscilla and me or maybe a few dates with Jonathan and Chrystal. But Mom's message was clear. *All of you. Together.*

With that said, we took the hardest season of our lives, in the midst of personal, national, and global tragedy, to come together and honor our mother's final wish. We are calling this ministry together Kingdom Legacy. It's our way of paying tribute to her strength, her legacy, her faithfulness to raise us day in and day out as servants, to impact people for the kingdom and to glorify God.

This is where we begin. Small steps and open conversations. Telling our story in the most authentic, transparent, and humble way possible. Asking the difficult questions, examining our faith. Is it stage faith, or is it real? What beauty can truly come from ashes? What does it mean to dig deep as life has broken our hearts?

Broken has become something of a cliché in Christian culture. We have lost loved ones, battled sickness, and struggled to make it through the toughest of days. We have sat in far too many doctors' offices, hospitals, and funeral homes. Praying, waiting, crying together and alone. Fighting through sleepless nights and anxious cross-country flights. Drinking bad coffee. Seems even our scars have scars. Broken is no cliché. We have all been hit so hard.

> **Life has been interrupted, but we have to believe there is a divine message in the disruption somehow. One that could save our lives and, ultimately, bring us closer to each other and God.**

The Evans family is not alone. The entire world is shaking. War, famine, fear, plague, civil unrest, financial loss, and family members dying. Even as I write these words, we are in the midst of a freak winter storm that has trapped Dallas under a blanket of snow and ice. Millions are without power and water, even sleeping in their cars to stay warm.

The regularly scheduled programming of our lives has been disrupted. Remember that? As a kid, it was always frightening (and frustrating) when the network would cut into one of my favorite TV shows with a news bulletin. In Texas that could mean tornadoes coming or gale winds, some man-made or natural disaster barreling down. But the message coming through was important. It just might save your life.

Life has been interrupted, but we have to believe there is a divine message in the disruption somehow. One that could save our lives and, ultimately, bring us closer to each other and God.

So, in starting ministry together, we invite you, the reader, in. Everybody together. My mother always liked that. She knew something was coming. Proverbs says that a good parent lays up treasure for generations to come. *All of you. Together. Trusting God.*

That's the only way through.

BEFORE WE BEGIN

Here we are, together, all four Evans kids and our dad, to talk about holding tight to faith when life has broken your heart.

This is a different kind of book. In it, you'll find our family's story of disruption, but because we are a family of pastors, teachers, preachers, and worship leaders, it's our nature to take what we have experienced and find the good. We hope you will learn and grow spiritually as we walk this road together, seeing God's hand through hard times.

What follows in part 1 are lots of stories we've never shared before, a little teaching and preaching, and then, in part 2, the tone becomes more devotional. But more importantly, it's all a conversation, like coming over to our family's house on a Saturday evening to sit around the table and talk about life, God, and how to keep moving in the face of enormous struggle and loss. Each of us will speak, and we pray that you find hope and unique perspective in our individual voices.

JONATHAN EVANS

And some of us might talk more than others. Just as if we were sitting around the table.

ANTHONY

That's Jonathan, my younger brother. To keep things clear, we'll label each family member before they speak. There will be a lot of back-and-forth, sometimes all five of us, sometimes only two. We've never done anything like this before. Actually, we're not sure anyone else has either.

PRISCILLA SHIRER

We have all been through hard seasons, times in life when it seems like the hits keep coming and you can barely catch your breath. Sometimes we look at Christians in the spotlight of public ministry and think they have some secret measure of faith, like they've figured out how to stay above the struggles of life. But no one is above them. We'd all love to find a way to go around trouble, but often you just have to walk through it. Our family has been through it. And we're going to walk you through with us, step-by-step.

> Sometimes we look at Christians in the spotlight of public ministry and think they have some secret measure of faith, like they've figured out how to stay above the struggles of life. But no one is above them.

CHRYSTAL EVANS HURST

I'm the oldest child and the processor of the family. Whenever we have conversations, I like to gather my thoughts completely before saying a word. I might come off as quiet at first, but I'm thinking and formulating exactly what I want to communicate.

If I've learned anything during this difficult time, it's that we are all in it together. I'm ridiculously aware of how much we need each other. I've never been through anything tougher. I don't think any of us have. I have also never been so grateful for my family.

So welcome to *Divine Disruption*. This is our very first published work as a family and the first ever Kingdom Legacy project. We're sharing our individual experiences, woven together, just as our life stories have been intertwined the last few years. We have been blessed and pray this legacy work blesses you too.

PART ONE

GOOD GOD, HARD TIMES

I will not cause pain
without allowing something new to be born, says the Lᴏʀᴅ.
—ISAIAH 66:9 ɴᴄᴠ

If there's one thing you can count on in your life,
it's that your path will not always be easy.
—DR. TONY EVANS

ONE

WYNTER IN JULY

The Lord is close to the brokenhearted
and saves those who are crushed in spirit.
—PSALM 34:18 NIV

PRISCILLA

July 24, 2018, was my nineteenth wedding anniversary, so my husband, Jerry, and I decided to go out to Clearfork in Fort Worth for our anniversary dinner. Afterward, we stopped at HomeGoods to buy a few things for the family. Apparently, that's what couples who've been married two decades do. Somehow even wandering down the aisles of a regular store seemed romantic that day.

I was halfway down the aisle with some washcloths and towels in my hand when my cell phone rang. I fumbled with it to quickly check the screen.

Jonathan Pitts

That's my cousin Wynter's husband. Growing up in the Evans family, first cousins are like another sibling. In fact, Wynter and I actually called each other sister-cousins. And beyond our biological connection, she and I were honest-to-goodness best friends.

Wynter, Jonathan, and their four daughters had been staying in our old house while preparing to transition to an exciting new season in life as God called them to ministry in Tennessee. I tapped the answer button.

"What's up, Pitts?" I said jokingly. My baby brother's name is Jonathan, too, so we call Wynter's husband Pitts.

No reply. "Pitts? You there?"

The deepest, most awful wail echoed through my phone. I froze, waiting. Finally, the words broke through.

"She's not breathing, Silla," he cried. "I don't think she's breathing."

"Who's not breathing?" I said.

Jerry turned to me, sensing something was horribly wrong from the tone of my voice.

"Wynter," Pitts replied. "She stopped breathing and . . . I don't think she's gonna make it." He kept on talking, but I couldn't make out the words for all his tears.

"Ambulance!" I shouted. "Did you call the ambulance?"

I looked to Jerry. He nodded back. I threw the towels on the shelf, and we started running for the car.

"We're on our way," I told Pitts.

I called our friends Tom and Rachel, who live next door to our old house, and frantically told them what was happening. Within three minutes they were with Jonathan, Wynter, and the girls.

It was a thirty-minute drive from where we had been celebrating to the part of town where Wynter and Pitts were staying. Silence in the car. Jerry reached over and took my hand.

"What if she doesn't make it?" he asked.

Wynter and I were tight as sisters, together at every step, high and low. I couldn't even imagine such a thing. We were still so young and had so many plans for our families and ourselves.

Soon I received a text letting us know she was being taken to the emergency room at Baylor University Medical Center, so we drove straight there. All four of Wynter's daughters were in the waiting room with Tom and Rachel when we arrived. We hugged each one, and I looked to Rachel to see if there were any updates on Wynter's condition. Rachel sadly shook her head.

I knew we were supposed to wait out front for further news, but I couldn't. It was unbearable. More than thirty minutes had passed since Pitts first called me, and Wynter was still not breathing? Did that mean breathing on her own? Did they insert a tube or put her on a ventilator or what? I stared at the locked door that led to the back of the emergency room, feeling helpless. And just then my dad walked in.

All right, enough, I thought. *We're doing something about this.*

DR. TONY EVANS

I was already in bed when the call came that my niece Wynter had been rushed to the hospital. I called Jonathan Pitts, and he said they were at the Baylor emergency room and Wynter still wasn't breathing. He was weeping.

"It doesn't look good," he said.

Pitts and I worked side by side in ministry, and Wynter was as close as one of my own daughters. Their kids even call me Poppy.

"I'll be right there," I told him. I got up, pulled on some clothes, and headed to the hospital.

Priscilla caught me as soon as I walked through the ER doors and somehow talked a nurse into letting us in the back. We walked into the room. Jonathan was sitting beside Wynter's bed with his head in his hands.

"She's gone," he said.

Then he said it again. And again. I felt the sadness, the shock, the heartache, seeing a young man sobbing over his thirty-eight-year-old wife. I put my arms around his shoulders, trying to offer comfort.

After a moment, he stood to hug Priscilla, and she helped him walk into the hallway to get some air. I stayed in the room with Wynter for a moment longer. Looking down at her, I was struggling to comprehend how something like this could happen to someone so full of life. It seemed only yesterday she was a tiny girl in my arms, teasing, laughing.

I reached out and touched her cooling hand.

Just a couple of weeks before, a friend of mine had been pronounced dead. While still on the exam table, as the family wailed, he began to twitch. They could not believe what they were seeing, and neither could the doctors, who had just called the time of death. Now, my friend was up, walking around, alive and well, praising the Lord. I have seen it with my own eyes. Something like that will jump-start your faith.

I laid hands on my niece and prayed, *God, you can turn this around right now.* Jesus wept, and Lazarus got up. Jairus's daughter died, and Jesus said, "*She is not dead, only sleeping.*"

Turn it around, Lord, I pleaded. *Please.*

My wife, Lois, arrived soon after. Family and church family began to stream into the lobby of Baylor Medical Center. Wynter's daughters came into a small room where Jonathan told them the devastating news. And then I watched a heartbroken father gather his girls into his arms and lead them in singing "Good Good Father" and several other songs of praise.

In all my years of ministry, it was one of the most incredible displays of spiritual maturity I have ever witnessed. In the midst of tragedy, there was trust. In the most painful moments, something beautiful was taking place. One by one, family

> In the midst of tragedy, there was trust. In the most painful moments, something beautiful was taking place.

members slipped into Wynter's room to say their last goodbyes. Pitts joined us and asked Priscilla to lead us in song. She thought a moment before choosing the old hymn "Victory in Jesus."

Lois slid her hand into mine, and we began to sing.

CHRYSTAL

I was at choir rehearsal. My phone was steadily buzzing, but I was in charge of the music for our upcoming women's conference, so I noticed the noise but didn't pick up. When the buzzing didn't stop, I finally looked down and realized the texts were all from Priscilla.

911 Call Immediately Please

I paused choir rehearsal long enough to call her back. My face was calm, but my heart beat faster as I anticipated what news might be on the other end of the call.

Priscilla didn't say much. She was vague. In normal, everyday life, Priscilla doesn't like to incite drama or unnecessarily excite people, so her voice was calm and steady, but I could tell that whatever was going on, it was bad. She told me I needed to come to the hospital and that something was wrong with Wynter. Immediately, I let the choir know I had an emergency and asked for their prayers. My cousin Faith was in the room, so I grabbed her, and we headed across town to Baylor.

On the way to the hospital, I prayed and asked God to help Wynter, that whatever emergency had caused her to be rushed to the ER would be alleviated as quickly and painlessly as possible. Sensing that it was worse than I could imagine, my prayers intensified. I asked God to cancel whatever arrow the Enemy had aimed at Wynter and her family and for a miracle, if that's what was needed. And I believed that He could do it.

Like Priscilla, I want to keep things calm, so I don't lead with my emotions. But it's more than that. I'm also processing. As I walked into the emergency room, my face was set, steady. Though waves of worry were rolling inside of me, the surface remained still.

Well, that was me until they led me back to the room and I saw Wynter lying there, so still. I knew the situation was serious, but I didn't know she was already gone. I stood there in disbelief, thinking she would wake up and start talking to me at any moment. I touched her. She was still warm.

It's strange what you notice in traumatic times. Wynter hated for anyone to touch her feet, so of course, being super-close first cousins, I would do it all the time, just to drive her nuts. It was our little inside joke. Grabbing her toes at opportune times and tickling the bottoms of her feet would unnerve her in the best of ways. It gave me a reason to laugh because I loved messing with her. I loved *her*.

Wynter loved to be cozy. And now she was lying in a hospital bed, wearing socks that I had bought for her. Blue socks, the soft, fuzzy kind, hugged her tiny feet. Wynter so loved those fuzzy blue socks. They went with her everywhere.

And now, under bright lights in a sterile cold room, she lay still.

In that moment, I no longer could be rational or calm. There was nothing to think through or process, nothing I could take charge of or change. When there's nothing I can do to make things happen, I am lost.

As the waves rolled to the surface, the tears did too.

JONATHAN

I was at home, having a normal day with my family. My wife, Kanika, and I were in the bedroom, wrestling with the kids, playing around. Kamden was climbing on my neck while Kylar hopped up into my lap. That's when Priscilla called.

"What are you doing?" she asked.

"Nothing, really. Just messing around with the kids and stuff," I replied. "Why?"

"Can you leave the room?"

I could hear the seriousness in her voice, so I jetted toward the kitchen.

"Wynter's on her way to the hospital," Priscilla said.

Poor little Wynt, I was thinking. *What'd she do? Stub her toe or something?* I was sure it was something minor. Wynter was thirty-eight, in the prime of her life, seemingly healthy in every way.

Silla's voice cracked as she continued. "Jon, they don't think she's going to make it."

A chill crept up my spine as I tried to process what I'd heard. "What's going on?"

"She's not breathing," Priscilla said. "They've got her in an ambulance headed to the ER at Baylor now."

Kanika must have sensed something was wrong because she came flying out of the room. I hung up and told her what was going on. We have four young children, so I was scrambling, trying to get in touch with our babysitter. The atmosphere in the house was chaotic, as the kids could tell there was trouble going down.

I got in touch with our sitter, told her we had a family emergency, and, thank God, she was able to come right over. She told us to go and not worry about what time we got back. Kanika and I jumped in the car and sped to the hospital, praying the whole way.

God, I know You're going to come through. I know You're going to make this happen. God, save Wynter. Heal her. Make it better, Lord.

Every prayer we could think of, we were sending up to God. By the time we pulled into the parking lot at Baylor, we were prayed up and hopeful, fully believing the Lord would come through. We felt certain Wynter would be awake and alert by the time we arrived, and we would all have a laugh. Like, *Girl, you almost died on us! What is wrong with you?* Whatever it was, the doctors would figure it out. God would fix it. Everything would be all right.

We were the last to make it to the emergency room. In the hallway, Wynter's daughters ran to meet us, crying, falling against our chests. Pitts came up, kneeled, and put his arms around them.

"Mama's going to be okay," he promised. "Jesus has her now."

Yes, amen! I thought. *The doctors are working it out. Jesus has got her. He's going to make all of this okay.*

We walked over to where the rest of the family was waiting. Everyone seemed too stunned to speak. Jerry, Priscilla's husband, finally told us the news.

"Wynter died," he said. "They're on their way to take her to the morgue now."

At that moment, the gurney passed, carrying her body. That's when the horrific reality hit. And that's when we completely fell apart.

ANTHONY

It was another fast-paced day in Los Angeles, traffic buzzing, projects pitched and planned, everything running in high gear. That's the way I like it, the life I love to live.

I had a meeting set up with a potential talent manager and was rushing to get dressed, get in the car, and head to a West Hollywood meeting spot, with all its vibed-out glam. I was racing down Sunset Boulevard when I saw the first text from Priscilla. *Catch you later, Silla,* I thought. *I'm already running late.* Then my phone rang, and it was Jerry.

I put it on speaker because it's illegal to hold your phone while driving in L.A. Jerry cut straight to the point. "Wynter's gone," he said.

"Wait, what? What do you mean, Jerry?" I asked, trying to process his words. They could not mean what I think he meant. So I said it again. "What do you mean?"

His tone was solemn. "Anthony," he said, "Wynter died. She's gone."

That's it. That was all there was to say. Explaining anything more would have been too hard in the moment. My fast-paced day stopped cold. I turned the car around and headed back to throw a bag together. Then I booked a flight and headed out for what felt like the longest ever flight home.

I sat in that tiny airplane seat with a blanket over my head, crying my eyes out, thinking, *This cannot be real.* Wynter and Jonathan Pitts are as close as my own brother and sisters. We had just been together for a Fourth of July weekend at the lake, and they were so excited. Wynter's writing career was growing, and Pitts had just been hired to a pastoral position at Church of the City in Franklin, Tennessee. Whatever else was going on in life, we all came together every month for a time of pure fellowship and fun, to bond, refresh, and catch up. Life is about family. Family and God. Everything else is just illusion.

Suddenly, the L.A. dream didn't mean much anymore.

I landed in Dallas late, so it was the next morning before I made it to my family. When I saw Pitts and the girls, we just fell into each other's arms. We cried and kept holding onto each other. It all felt so surreal, like being stuck in a really bad dream.

There was nothing to say, no words. The only thing that could be done at that point was to be there.

I had never really dealt with anything like this before. I didn't lose my grandfather until I was twenty-eight years old. I suppose our family had been blessed.

PRISCILLA

We were at the hospital until well after midnight, consoling each other. Then we slept a few hours before heading back to Jonathan and the girls to offer whatever help we could. It was Wednesday, which meant that we had a night service at church to figure out. As usual, Dad was scheduled to finish up a sermon series. Even though Wynter was like a daughter to him, I know my father, and I knew he planned to show up and preach like he always did.

My siblings and I knew that word had started to get out about Wynter's passing.

"Dad, you can't just preach like nothing happened," we told him. "People are going to know. Would you consider suspending your series and addressing what happened instead? It could be a great help to others who are experiencing unexpected loss and grief. Let tonight's service be about that."

We also knew the only way to get Dad into a conversational style, where he'd share the disappointment and pain he was feeling, would be if all of us were on the platform together, sitting next to him and asking him questions about trusting God during difficult times. No pulpit, no podium, no traditional preaching. We had been on the go for more than twenty-four hours by this point and hadn't had time to shower or change clothes, but we decided that "come as you are" applied to our situation.

> How can we reconcile the kindness of God when He allows such difficult things? What do you do when you are disappointed with God?

At 7:00 p.m. we drove to church and walked onstage in flip-flops and jeans, grungy gym clothes, tennis shoes, and hair pulled back into a ponytail. The four kids with Daddy, asking questions, talking about tragedy and unexpected loss. How can we reconcile the kindness of God when He allows such difficult things? What do you do when you are disappointed with God? How does Dr. Tony Evans handle it when something like this happens?

I thought it would be healthy for the church to see their pastor talk about pain in such a personal way, not as a great and gifted preacher, but simply as a human being struggling to comprehend heartbreak. He has always been viewed as a superhero of the faith. But none of us are superheroes all the time. We hurt and struggle and fall and get back up again. Only by grace and God's help do we find the strength.

TWO

GOD KNOWS WHAT HE'S DOING

Teach us to number our days,
that we may gain a heart of wisdom.
—PSALM 90:12 NIV

TONY

I struggle with wanting to minister to everyone when a crisis hits and letting that overshadow my own feelings. Obviously, there are people hurting more than I. Four young girls lost their mother; a husband is grieving his wife.

But I do hurt. I hurt. People come to my office and want to give up because life has become too hard. I know they are coming to me and looking for hope. A good shepherd takes care of the sheep. But I also have to be strong enough to try to offer hope when I am hurting too.

The sudden loss of a loved one is something everybody faces or will face at some time. Besides, we had been talking about some intensely emotional issues at the church around that time. It would be hard to stick to the regularly scheduled sermon series while we were in the midst of a crisis that could have such a spiritual influence and impact on the congregation.

So I looked at that Wednesday-night church service as a *kairos* moment, an opportune time to reflect on God's heart, offer authenticity, and point to the hope we have in Jesus. It would allow us to express what we were dealing with and ask our church family to pray for the Pitts family.

> We pray, *Let this cup pass from me.* But we have to believe that God knows what He is doing when He's not doing what we want Him to do.

There was confusion with me. How could this happen to someone who appeared to be a healthy thirty-eight-year-old mother, especially in light of the new plans the Lord had brought into their lives and the new vision they were sharing? And so it raises the question, How do you balance the goodness of God with the tragedies of life?

My son Jonathan took the microphone and asked me, "Dad, how do you keep going?"

"Because I believe what I preach," I responded. "Where would I be in a situation like this without an anchor? I believe Wynter is in a better place. I believe in the sovereignty and goodness of God. And because I believe, I keep going."

The Bible is full of questions, people asking why. Why do the righteous suffer? That's the theme of the entire book of Job. How do I make sense of this? How could this happen? Why?

I cannot answer that. Deuteronomy 29:29 says God has secret things, that He does not have to answer our every question. That is His prerogative. But I would tell Wynter's children this: Your mother loved the Lord. And the Lord loved your mother. So, in some way beyond our understanding, He determined it was her time. I don't like it, and you don't like it. We pray, *Let this cup pass from me.* But we have to believe that God knows what He is doing when He's not doing what we want Him to do.

JONATHAN

I am the most frustrated when I come up against something I have no control over. Death and timing belong to God, and He doesn't allow me into that space. All I can do is trust that God knows what He is doing. My father tells me this, and I am a father, too, so I know it is true. There are things fathers must do that their children cannot understand. That's what trust is.

ANTHONY

Priscilla told me that Daddy had agreed to do the Wednesday-night service, so that's what we did. We all went to the church. The tech team handed each of us a microphone, and together we walked up the few steps to the platform. Chrystal, Priscilla, Jonathan, and I sat beside Dad.

We all have unique personalities when crises hit. Chrystal is quiet and deep. Jonathan gets logical. Priscilla becomes a caretaker. My dad goes straight to faith, straight to God's Word. Me? I am the super-sensitive member of the Evans family. I go directly to emotions.

I sat quietly as Dad talked about clinging to God in hard times. I wanted to support my family, but I was upset. *Why are we sitting on stage at church? Not even twenty-four hours after tragedy hits, and we're up here talking about it in public.* I didn't feel like we owed that to anyone. I didn't feel like anybody would expect it so soon. So when it was my turn to speak, I told the truth about how I felt.

"If I were not in this family, I would have been gone a long time ago," I confessed. "Because this kind of stuff throws me way off. If you're like me, when you lose a family member that is so close, that you are so connected to, and you race to their side and hold her young daughters as they cry, and they look up to you and ask, 'Uncle Nene, why?' And you are so full of rage because you *cannot* believe this is happening. It wasn't because of something evil. Wynter's heart stopped. I feel like God allowed that to happen. So, honestly? I cannot go to hope and faith so quickly. Right now, I am just mad."

What do you do when you are not built like Dr. Tony Evans, the great theologian? Even though we share the same name, even though I should be thankful for the breath in my lungs, even knowing God does not owe me anything. How do I process my feelings of betrayal and anger? I can't immediately start quoting Bible verses. First, I have to process the pain.

Thank God, I have always been able to bounce things off my parents, to tell it to them straight. Dad told me it was okay to be angry, as long as we do not allow anger to cause us to sin or turn our heart against God. In that moment, the vulnerability, the authenticity of being able to express my anger and confusion, to say it out loud, over a microphone, to all the church members gathered that night—there was freedom just in that simple expression.

> Dad told me it was okay to be angry, as long as we do not allow anger to cause us to sin or turn our heart against God.

Owning my anger was the beginning of understanding that Jesus is still with me, even in grief. We don't have to get everything resolved before we come to God.

PRISCILLA

After Anthony spoke so honestly, there was a smattering of soft applause. "I wonder," I said, "since Anthony is willing to be so honest, who here has ever felt the same way?"

Hands went up all across the room.

Truth is, I felt that way too. Wynter had so much life left to live. We had so many discussions about what our lives could look like once our children were grown. There were trips to take and adventures we intended to have. She was such a gifted writer and speaker, passionate about outreach to young girls, excited to move to Nashville and take the next step in her ministry. Wynter had been incredibly productive in recent years, casting vision for an effective girls ministry and writing books that were blessing thousands of people. She was in the middle of a new writing project and was so excited about that. Through it all, she never let ambition derail her from staying focused on God, loving her husband, and prioritizing her children—and never missing the opportunity to take one of her treasured afternoon naps.

And she always made time for family and friends. Our favorite thing was to slip off for movie night and get lost in a mountain of popcorn, talking, laughing, acting silly. But our conversation could turn deep in an instant. Her welcoming voice was low and raspy, soothing like the first warm cup of morning coffee. The words she shared always came from a place of intuition and peace. There wasn't anything I couldn't tell her. Wynter was my very best friend. I could not understand why a loving God would decide to take her home.

TONY

Jesus was baptized by His cousin John, and not a year later, King Herod had John thrown into a cruel prison. A devious woman danced for the king, a deal was made, and John the Baptist was brutally executed. Christ was fully God yet fully man. He lost a beloved cousin too.

This shows me that we can be angry but still respectful. It's okay to feel the pain of God disappointing us. God already knows how we feel. Hiding it doesn't help. We can take our anger to Him.

We've also got to have the right theology of death, an eternal perspective. Otherwise, death can only be viewed as destructive. In God's economy, He makes an astounding statement in Psalm 116:15:

> It's okay to feel the pain of God disappointing us. God already knows how we feel. Hiding it doesn't help.

"Precious in the sight of the LORD is the death of his faithful servants" (NIV). And Paul said in 2 Corinthians 5:8, "To be absent from the body [is] to be present with the Lord" (KJV). The body remains, but the soul is very much alive.

Wynter now lives with God. And God is excited about that.

The seventh chapter of Ecclesiastes tells us that it's better to go to a funeral than a party because only at a funeral do we take life seriously. In good times, no one thinks about the end. We are laughing and having fun. That's good, but at a funeral, we face the important things in life: family, love, and the legacy we leave behind. At funerals, we are faced with perspective. "Death is the destiny of everyone," King Solomon promised in verse 2, "the living should take this to heart" (NIV).

In Psalm 90:12, King David recorded a prayer of Moses: "Teach us to number our days, that we may gain a heart of wisdom" (NIV). No one numbers their days at a wedding party. But at a funeral home? I am in my seventies now. I do not know where the time went. Seems just yesterday I was turning thirty-five. Time goes so fast.

CHRYSTAL

If you get rid of God, you still have your problems. Sickness and evil still exist. The disciples doubted; they struggled with faith in the face of loss and fear. The Bible says many of them turned away and no longer followed Christ.

In John 6:67–68, Jesus said to those who remained, "Do you want to leave, too?"

"Lord, who would we go to?" the apostle Peter replied. "You have the words that give eternal life" (NCV).

We have not solved our problems by running from God. The goodness of God is all around us. It only comes into question when bad things happen. So, now, when facing tragedy, we question God.

But what about all the days when there were no questions, when we were laughing and celebrating life? We have to put the sorrow and pain against the history of God's goodness.

How can a good God allow evil? That is the question of theodicy, the virtue of God versus the reality of evil. God has given us a choice. Joshua 24:15 says, "If serving the LORD seems undesirable to you, then choose for yourselves this day whom you will serve" (NIV).

With choice, the potential for evil exists because we can choose against the good. Freedom allows evil to exist, but we make evil happen. Choices have consequences. The decisions we make affect others.

That is why we need a sovereign God who can at least choose to intervene in the reality of evil in this world. If I am left to other people, then I'm subject to anything anybody wants to do, anytime they want to do it. But if I have God, then evil has to flow through His fingers before it can get to me. Even when things seem out of control, I have hope that God is in control.

For believers, the present is not life. This is only an introduction to life.

Like Peter, I ask, Where else could I go? If you take that away from me, I have no hope. I would rather cast my life with a God I don't understand than with people.

For believers, the present is not life. This is only an introduction to life. If we keep that in mind while expressing our honesty to God, we can keep the right perspective in our pain. We can offer praise in the midst of our tears. Like the apostle Paul, we can pray at midnight while still in chains.

When the storm is raging, trust God.

---- **THREE** ----

A NEW NORMAL

Therefore we will not be afraid,
though the earth trembles
and the mountains topple
into the depths of the seas,
though its water roars and foams
and the mountains quake with its turmoil. *Selah*

—PSALM 46:2-3

PRISCILLA

In March 2019, Dad was inducted into the National Religious Broadcasters' Hall of Fame at the annual Christian Media Convention held that year in Anaheim, California. We were all so incredibly proud. According to the program that night, the NRB Hall of Fame stands as "a showcase of warriors for Christ who have lived exemplary lives of valor and compassion, blazing trails and leaving paths for succeeding generations to follow. NRB's most prestigious award is presented . . . for invaluable contribution to the field of Christian communications, exhibition of the highest standards and evidence of faithfulness in Christ."

That's my father. He has worked so hard and been so faithful. My siblings, Mom, and I all flew out to Anaheim for his big night.

Once we arrived, Dad seemed preoccupied, always tied up on the phone in another room. Obviously, something was heavy on his mind. By contrast, Mom was lighthearted, but the dynamic still felt uneasy and strained. Something didn't seem quite right. NRB is always fun for my parents, catching up with old friends and making plans for the future of the ministry and the broadcast. When you have been in ministry for more than thirty years, this annual gathering is like a big high school reunion. And here Dad was, being honored for his exceptional work, but he did not seem to be enjoying it one bit.

At one point, Jonathan and I both had eyes on Dad. "Something seem wrong with Daddy to you?" I asked.

"Yeah," Jonathan said. "I see it too."

We walked over to him. "Dad, are you excited?" I asked, fishing for some clue of what the problem might be. "Tomorrow's your big day."

"We'll get there when we get there," he replied dryly.

"What's wrong? Are you all right?"

"Fine, I'm fine," he said, flashing that thousand-watt Tony Evans smile. "We'll talk about it later."

Jonathan shot me a look. We weren't buying it, but Dad is Dad. If something was bothering him, we figured he would let us know soon enough.

Friday rolled around. Jonathan knocked on my door early in the morning and grabbed my hand to snatch me out of the room. I was still in my pajamas, but so were Chrystal and Anthony, who joined us as we ran through the hotel hallway like kids on Christmas morning. I banged on the door to Mom and Dad's room. He opened it to let us in.

"It's Friday, Dad!" I said. "Tonight you're going to be inducted into the NRB Hall of Fame!"

No response. He just nodded while Mom patted him on the shoulder.

"Daddy, what is wrong?" I asked. Again, he did not answer.

Later that night, we all got dressed to the nines. Banquets and ceremonies can be a bit stuffy, but when the Evans family gets together, there's always going to be some laughs and clowning around. At least at our table.

Mom had a smile on. Dad's old friends were stopping by the table to congratulate him on the award. He was pleasant but stoic, nowhere near his usual jovial self. We were all shooting looks back and forth at that point, wondering what could be on our father's mind.

JONATHAN

Dad should be on the mountaintop, but he's stuck in the valley instead. I walked around to his side of the table and stooped down, close to his ear. "Dad," I asked, resting my hand on his shoulder. "Are you going to be okay?"

"I love you, Jon Jon," he replied, avoiding the question.

"I love you, too, Daddy."

They called his name from the stage and announced the honor. He went up and did what I've always known my dad to do: preach a powerful, gospel-filled message about the will of God, His Word, and how the Lord can make a miracle from a mess.

PRISCILLA

Dad received the award, posed for pictures, and shook hands with all those who came to congratulate him. We rushed to his side as soon as the induction was done. Family pictures, platform pictures, greenroom pictures. So many pictures that it felt like the paparazzi had descended on the convention center. This should have been one of the happiest days in our family's history. But for some reason, it was not. We were posing for another picture, all of us kids gathered around my father as he held his award high. After the camera flashed, I grabbed his sleeve.

"Dad, come on now," I pleaded. "You're always excited at NRB. You just got inducted into the hall of fame, and the whole night you've had a grimace on your face. Please tell us what's going on."

"Meet me in my room in ten minutes," he said, "and I'll tell you."

CHRYSTAL

I knew right then, something was up.

JONATHAN

We all did. You talk about four hearts pounding. All of the hairs on my arm took flight.

PRISCILLA

We changed clothes and headed straight to Mom and Dad's room. It took me a bit longer to get my kids situated, so I was the last to arrive. When I walked in, the room was solemn.

"Okay, now we can start," Dad said, nodding to me. "Let's go."

I took a seat next to Mom.

"Kids, your mother felt a little knot on her side a couple of weeks ago," he began. "So she went to the doctor, and they performed a scan. Her cancer has returned."

Whatever air was in the room was sucked out in that moment. I reached over and grabbed my mother's hand. She wasn't tearful or upset. In fact, she was smiling calmly in a way that seemed to say, *It is what it is.*

"We are still believing God for healing," my father added. "But medically, there's nothing they can do."

JONATHAN

I was not able to process what Dad was saying at the time. I was too numb.

"She's in stage four," he explained. "The tumor has spread all the way across her abdomen. I've talked to the best doctors. I've gone high, and I've gone low. I have gone everywhere in-between, and there is absolutely nothing they can do about it. So if I've been somber all week, it's because we are facing the hardest time we've ever faced in our family."

Dad dropped the hammer on us. Mommy had cancer, and it was terminal. Even after we were grown, my siblings and I still called her "Mommy." She never stopped mothering, mentoring, and caring for us.

27

PRISCILLA

Let me explain something about our father. He's a fixer. Faith in action. Let's make a plan, come up with solutions. That has always been Dad's love language with my mother. He fixes things. Whatever it is, he takes care of it.

> Dad dropped the hammer on us. Mommy had cancer, and it was terminal.

Mom finally spoke. "They're not saying I'm going to die soon or anything like that," she said. "They haven't given me a time." The room was silent. "I want you all to trust God with this season of my life. I am."

Opening the Notes app on her phone, Mom began to read a few Scriptures she'd been keeping close to her heart. She told us, in no uncertain terms, that her illness should not stop the ministry from going forward, that the Enemy would take too much pleasure in our discouragement and defeat. She talked about trusting God and moving forward.

All of a sudden, from the other side of the room, a wail broke out, piercing the silence and sending a chill through our hearts. It was Dad. Up until that time I had witnessed my father shed tears maybe twice in my life. He didn't even cry openly at his parents' funerals. But that day, he began to weep and cry out, "Oh, God. Oh, God."

We were all shocked. None of us had ever seen our father break down this way. We ran to him and threw our arms around him. That's when we all began to cry.

CHRYSTAL

To see my father not just get tearful but totally fall apart meant things were truly bad. This was a problem he could not fix. It was also why he had been on the phone so much. Dad was on a mission. He'd been calling everyone he could, any connection, anyone who might know of an experimental treatment or a clinical trial—anything that might save our mom. If my father had already turned over every rock, because he is that kind of guy, then apart from some raging miracle . . . I honestly could not bring myself to put into words the reality of what we were facing.

And then to look over at my mother, with the same level of stillness and peace she had the whole weekend, right then and there I started losing her. I hugged Mommy before we left the room and held on to her for a really long time. There was nothing to say or do in that moment, nothing except to hold on.

TONY

Just before NRB, Lois discovered a knot on the opposite side from where her gallbladder had been removed and had it biopsied. It was a cancerous tumor. As I studied her condition, I discovered how aggressive the cancer was. I felt totally helpless because the survival rate is low, especially once it spreads across the stomach. I knew we were dealing with a serious issue. The weight of the diagnosis was so very heavy to bear. Then to have to share the news with our children? It was nearly intolerable.

ANTHONY

I remember staring out the hotel window feeling completely blank. Our family is so used to taking action. When a problem comes up, we jump into figuring out a plan for attack. So when we heard that the end had already been determined, that medically there was no solution to Mom's problem, we felt helpless. There was nothing we could do.

My first clear thought was to figure out some way to help with the heartache and mental stress I knew my father had been going through. Mommy always took the high road and put her struggles aside to make sure we were all okay, but I knew that underneath her calm, collected smile, she had to be hurting too. My parents had always taken care of me. Now, I wanted to care for them.

Still, once I got over the initial shock, the smallest inkling of hope began to rise up inside of me. *There's gotta be something the doctors can do for Mommy. They just haven't found it yet.*

JONATHAN

We were all a wreck in that hotel room. But there was one person who was not crying. My mother.

"All of you," she said, waving us in. "Come here and listen." She looked each one of us in the eye before speaking. "You do know what this is, don't you? It's called spiritual warfare. So much death and sickness has attacked our family lately. We must be doing something right because the Enemy is taking notice. God is allowing these things to happen. He's allowing things to be shaken up. I understand that you are sad, and I know it hurts to hear this news. But when the Enemy comes against our family, we will not tuck our tails and run. We prepare to attack. If you're called to preach, you will preach. If you're called to write, you will write. If you're called to sing, you will sing. Now, I have every expectation that you will love and care and pray for me and be there when I need you. But God has an expectation too. Always remember, through thick and through thin, that you are here to serve the purposes of God."

Her words were a lot to grasp at the time. Our heads were still spinning.

"Mom, how can you be talking about ministry at a time like this?" I asked.

"Because that's why you're here, son," she said. "It's the reason you exist."

She looked us all over again. "So you will stand up, hold your head up, and be strong. And you will continue the work of the ministry."

> Always remember, through thick and through thin, that you are here to serve the purposes of God.

CHRYSTAL

We left my parents' room and walked back slowly to the sound of our footsteps on the hotel carpet and sighs of restless unbelief. Finally, Anthony spoke up.

"What do we do?" he asked.

No one knew what to say. We stood at the elevators waiting, still silent. Each of us got off on our respective floors and went to bed. I woke up the next morning thinking that maybe the warm sun across my face would reveal all this to be a bad dream. But as the morning haze faded, I realized, *This really happened. It wasn't a nightmare. This is our new reality.*

FOUR

MOVE A LITTLE CLOSER

For our struggle is not against flesh and blood,
but against the rulers, against the authorities,
against the cosmic powers of this darkness,
against evil, spiritual forces in the heavens.
—EPHESIANS 6:12

TONY

I was sitting in my den this morning, looking through old pictures, thinking about good times, hard times, all the things Lois and I have gone through together over forty-nine years of marriage. Forty of those years we spent in this same house. We raised our children here. So many meals around the table, holding hands in prayer.

All four of our kids love and serve the Lord in ministry. I believe wholeheartedly that the next generation of my family will carry on to even greater things. This season has been hard. But it has brought us closer to each other and closer to God.

On this morning, I was thinking back to how Lois and I met. It was August 1968. I had traveled to Guyana, South America, as part of Sam Hart's Grand Old Gospel Fellowship Ministries.

Lois' parents, James and Annie Cannings, hosted our team, and we were able to spend a bit of time together. Lois sang and played the piano and did some traveling ministry herself. She was something else, a little reserved at times, but at her core, so outgoing and full of spark. And, oh, man, could she ever cook. I had never tasted food like that in my life. Fried chicken (my favorite!) and well-seasoned potatoes, the windows of heaven thrown open, blessings overflowing.

I flew back to the United States ten pounds heavier and certain that she was the girl God had sent for me. But it would be six months before I would make it back to Guyana to see her again.

After that short visit, I wrote letters to Lois every single day. That was the only way to keep in touch back then. International phone calls cost way more than a teenage preacher could afford. We couldn't even dream of a world with email, Zoom, or texting. So I got a pen, sat down, and poured out my feelings on paper. Every day. I even wrote a letter to her father upon my return to South America, asking for his daughter's hand in marriage.

I didn't get an answer right away, but Lois did move to America to continue her studies, which was common in that day. At least it was a step in the right direction. I was excited to have her in the States.

Lois was so lovely that I could not take my eyes off of her. But truth is, initially, she did not respond at the rate to which I was accustomed. Girlfriend was moving a little slow. I was sure she was the one God wanted me to marry, but I felt like I needed to help Him along a little bit. What I'm saying is, if our relationship was going to move forward at a faster clip, I knew I would have to help a sister out.

One night I called Lois and asked her to go with me to the Gwynn Oak Amusement Park. Nights are cold in Baltimore, and when the wind churned up off Gwynn Falls, well, it might cause a young couple to huddle tight. The park had hot chocolate, cotton candy, and thrill rides, like the Big Dipper and the Whip. My favorite was a roller coaster called the Wild Mouse.

The Wild Mouse did all the typical dips and turns, but there was one part where it shot down a straight piece of track, banked hard into a turn, and you really felt as if the car was going to jump off the tracks and crash down onto the midway.

I led Lois straight to it. "Two tickets, please," I said.

We climbed in and buckled the flimsy seat belt. Safety measures were a whole lot looser back then. The seats were snug, but the car sat wide on the skinny track, so as we climbed higher, it seemed like we were hanging perilously over the side.

At the first tall drop, Lois screamed and grabbed on tightly to my arm. *Yes, Lord*, I agreed. The wilder that mouse got, the closer Lois slid to me, and when we hit that hairpin curve, she pressed into me, head on my shoulder. *Hallelujah!* I declared.

By the time we circled back to the station, you couldn't have slid a butterknife between us. And the rest, as they say, is history.

On June 27, 1970, Lois Cannings became Mrs. Tony Evans. Our adventures had only begun.

I've been thinking about that Wild Mouse roller-coaster ride a lot lately in this season of hard dips and unexpected turns. See, the sudden movement and unexpected turns of that roller coaster made Lois slide closer to me, and life is often exactly like that. Sometimes God allows discomfort and distress because He wants us to move in close to Him. We don't cling to God nearly as much in carefree times, when things are smooth. We run to God when things are frightening or tough.

PRISCILLA

Six months before Wynter's death, Dad lost his younger brother. Arthur Evans Jr., Uncle Bo, was the picture of strength, always so full of laughter, life, and personality. Even though he had been battling bone cancer, it never seemed to slow him down. He stayed active right up to the end. It was a shock when he went downhill so quickly.

> **Sometimes God allows discomfort and distress because He wants us to move in close to Him.**

We all traveled to Florida to be by his side. Seven cousins, including Wynter, spent many memorable hours with him, talking and asking questions about his life. Uncle Bo knew he wasn't going to live much longer, and he was at peace with God. He passed just a week after our visit. We held Uncle Bo's funeral on a cold, dreary day in Baltimore. It was heartbreaking for Dad to bury his baby brother.

TONY

Bo was so competitive. We always had a good-natured, big brother–little brother rivalry going. I got my doctorate, and Bo made sure he got his too. After I led the prayer at our father's eighty-fifth birthday, Bo got up and said an even longer prayer, with more elaborate words. Then he shot me a look like, *Top that, big brother!*

ANTHONY

Our Uncle Bo was for sure our hilarious, fun uncle. He was always making us crack up, even in church. Dad would be preaching some profound message, getting all hermeneutical and theologically deep, thousands of people hanging on his every word. Uncle Bo would lean over to me and joke, "You know he doesn't have a clue what he's talking about, right?"

Wynter was there with us for Uncle Bo's last days. Little did we know that would be the last time all of the Evans cousins would come together that way. Thank God we all took a picture. It was hardly half a year later, the next summer, that Wynter was gone. Six months after Wynter's death, my father's sister, our beloved Aunt Beverly, passed away unexpectedly in January 2019 from a lung condition.

TONY

Beverly was the only girl in our family *and* the youngest. My parents spoiled that child. Later in life she became Mom and Dad's main caretaker, so she spoiled them right back. I lost my baby brother and sister one right after the other. With Bo, we knew it was coming. But Beverly's death was such a shock.

ANTHONY

The family rallied again for Aunt Beverly's funeral. It was an all-out celebration, high church choir. You should have seen the fancy hats across the sanctuary that morning! She was a detail-oriented lady and intently committed to her church, so it was all of the things she loved.

Aunt Beverly and I shared a birthday, so we had a special bond. She knew I was the sensitive kid in the family and always looked for ways to build me up. I thought we had a lot more years together.

You think, surely this is the end. Three funerals back-to-back-to-back. It's over, right?

Reality kept on beating us down. Aunt Beverly's husband, Uncle James, passed away shortly after we got the news about Mom's cancer returning. I think he was just holding on until Aunt Beverly passed. Once she was gone, it seemed that he lost the will to live. He loved her so much. And we loved him. Uncle James was good to us. We gathered up and headed off to yet another family funeral.

And then our beloved grandfather, Two Daddy, started to struggle more. I feel like this book should be titled *And Then . . .* because it seemed like it was one relentless thing after another.

A Celebration of Legacy

PRISCILLA

Two Daddy is the loving name we call Dad's dad, Arthur "Two Daddy" Evans. Even though Two Daddy was ninety, he was still upbeat and active, enjoying life. We traveled to Baltimore frequently to spend time with him, eating steamed Maryland crabs, driving him around town, and playing long, detailed games of checkers. He was sharp and lively. But then, in the fall of 2019, he started slowing down and not eating as much. Losing two children so soon, I think the emotional toll was hefty.

Beverly had been Two Daddy's primary caregiver before she passed away, so now Dad was having to watch over his dad's case as well. In addition to keeping the local church ministry strong, cultivating his own spiritual life, and supporting Mom's health journey, he now needed to attend to his father, who lived many states away. To say he had a lot on his plate would be an understatement.

We all jumped in to help, hoping that it would take some of the weight off of our dad. Chrystal and I spent most weeknights at our parents' home to support and care for them. Also, we began to help with the church in a more practical, hands-on way as Dad pushed some ministry projects back so he could prioritize his wife and father. But truth is, ministry is my father's life. Serving people and building the church are his lifeline and joy.

As time passed, Dad continued to make the necessary concessions. He made a commitment to be at every medical appointment and treatment with Mom, and he spent hours each day by her side whenever she met with doctors and nurses. As her treatment regimen ramped up, he let go of more things at work. That was his way of telling Mom, *I've got you.*

Cancer patients and their families know that treatment consumes your life. Your whole focus centers on keeping your loved one alive.

We all pitched in, and Anthony spent a lot of time traveling back to Texas to help. Those were some sweet family times together, taking Mom to appointments, spending nights with her, going to her favorite restaurants. Trials bring blessings too.

Cancer patients and their families know that treatment consumes your life. Your whole focus centers on keeping your loved one alive. That was true of us. It was bitter but sweet at the same time. We were all working together to get my mother better and keep the family and ministry afloat.

FIVE

BETWEEN EXPECTANCY AND REALITY

Do not fear, for I have redeemed you;
I have called you by your name; you are mine.
When you pass through the waters,
I will be with you,
and the rivers will not overwhelm you.
When you walk through the fire,
you will not be scorched,
and the flame will not burn you.
For I am the LORD your God,
the Holy One of Israel, and your Savior.

—ISAIAH 43:1–3

PRISCILLA

In July 2019, I went to the Cooper Clinic in Dallas for my annual physical. Three years earlier they had spotted a small irregular nodule in my lung, so they were monitoring it closely to determine if it could be scar tissue or an infection.

At the end of the comprehensive physical, the doctor sits with you to go through your test results. This time my doctor paused before speaking.

"Well, Priscilla, your CT scan is showing something the radiologists and doctors feel a little concerned about. The spot that we've been watching has grown. You need to see a pulmonary specialist immediately."

I nodded but could feel myself zoning out, unable to digest any more bad news.

My doctor continued. "I don't want you to be frightened, but I think you need to take it seriously. Anything that's growing and changing in your body is not good."

The appointments that August stacked up quickly. Pulmonary specialist, pulmonary surgeon, more scans and tests, everything back-to-back. One day I sat with Mom at her chemotherapy treatment on the second floor of Baylor Hospital. Immediately afterward, she and Dad accompanied Jerry and me to an appointment with my lung doctor on the third floor. All we did was switch offices. It almost seemed like a joke—the most obnoxious, unfunny joke ever—but nobody was laughing. I knew my situation would only add to my family's burden, and we were already so overwhelmed. With each appointment, the warning alarm about my health grew louder. I am generally a calm, even-tempered person, but so much trouble was raining down that I began to feel a persistent sting of panic. Like, *Oh, Lord, what's next?*

In the midst of all of this, we remained engaged in our individual ministries. Although my commitments were scaled down considerably, I was still showing up at speaking engagements and slowly working toward a publishing deadline that I'd already pushed back several times. My mother's words gave all of us momentum: *Keep going. The Enemy would take too much pleasure in our discouragement and defeat.* Despite the way we felt, we refused to cave in to fear, anxiety, or a decrease in faith.

My PET scan had come back negative. *Thank God*, I thought. *Finally, some good news.* However, my doctor said he could not tell me exactly what was growing in my lung.

"Just because your PET scan is negative doesn't mean that the growth isn't cancer," he continued. "There is a slow-growing cancer that doesn't have symptoms or show up on scans. Although I'm not certain, I suspect this is what you have. Unfortunately, because the mass is so deeply embedded in the center of your lung, we'll have to remove the entire upper lobe of your left lung in order to get it out."

I was stunned. Good news canceled. So many ugly words. *Mass. Remove. Entire upper lobe. Cancer.*

> My mother's words gave all of us momentum: *Keep going. The Enemy would take too much pleasure in our discouragement and defeat.*

I looked over to Mom. She put her head down, folded her arms, and balled up, shrinking into herself like a little girl as if she could not believe this was happening. Dad reached over, touching her leg.

"Lois, are you okay?" he asked.

In that moment, none of us were okay.

Mom and Dad asked the surgeon a lot of questions. I asked a lot of questions. He couldn't give any solid answers, only that the mass was dangerously irregular and had to come out. That was the only way to know the extent of the danger. And because of where it was, they would have to take one of the two lobes of my left lung along with it.

"But she's a preacher," Mom insisted. "She needs her lungs."

I smiled at Mom, even chuckling a bit at her comment. She was right. I did need my lungs to preach.

"If she were your daughter, what would you do?" Dad asked the doctor.

The surgeon was direct. "Schedule surgery. As soon as we possibly can."

We set my surgery for the first week in December 2019. Honestly, I didn't think much about it because we were all so focused on Mom. I don't like to make a big fuss about anything, so I did not discuss my diagnosis publicly. The journey was between Jerry, my immediate family, and me. I kept my chin up and, like Mom said, kept pressing into God's calling for me.

CHRYSTAL

Around this same time I, too, went for a doctor's appointment. During the examination an abnormal growth was found in my leg. Cancer had already hit so many of our family members that it was hard not to fear the worst. There were tests and scans with long nights of worry while I waited for the doctor to call.

For me, it turned out to be a false alarm, but for a while I was like, *Lord, what is the deal? Are you trying to put Daddy in the suffering hall of fame with Job?*

PRISCILLA

Mom and I spent a lot of time together that fall, even doing some shopping one day when she was feeling well enough to go. By that point she had lost forty pounds and was down to a size six. Nothing in her closet fit, and there were some events coming up that she was looking forward to attending.

Mom and Dad's seventieth birthdays were approaching, so of course, the church and family had plans to celebrate. Anthony was also planning Kingdom Legacy Live, an exciting event at Oak Cliff Bible Fellowship to commemorate the historic release of the Tony Evans Bible Commentary and Study Bible—a huge accomplishment.

ANTHONY

Dad is the first African American in history to write a study Bible and full commentary. More than fifty years of study and preaching are captured in its two thousand pages.

TONY

Throughout my ministry I've had an emphasis on the kingdom of God as the compass for the life of believers. My publisher thought this perspective would be a unique way to approach the Bible, and they suggested a commentary and study Bible along these lines would be helpful tools.

It took several years of accumulating decades of preaching and teaching materials. We even brought out the old cassette tapes. Night after night I worked into the early morning hours, rewriting old passages and creating new content as I summarized every paragraph of the Bible in a way that was relevant, clear, and kingdom-minded. It was a massive project, the biggest and most extensive of my life. When I finished editing the last version, I was glad it was done. Honestly, I don't think I want to take on a project that big ever again. It took every ounce of concentration and energy I had. But the Lord blessed it, and I am grateful to have done it.

But even as this history was in the making, the person who walked by my side every step of the way and helped me through it was Lois. And now she was suffering so much.

PRISCILLA

We were praying that Mom would feel good enough to attend Kingdom Legacy Live and the birthday celebrations planned for her and Dad.

She was going to need new clothes for all of these events, so I took Mom to her favorite department store in Dallas. If an outfit didn't fit her, she would make me try it on. We laughed a lot that afternoon, sharing a dressing room like two excitable teens. Afterward, we had a wonderful meal and rich conversation. It was the last shopping trip with Mom that I would ever take.

All summer and into the fall of 2019, Mom had more and more doctor visits because she added holistic options as well. One day, while a practitioner was running some tests, he told us that it looked like the tumors were getting smaller.

Mom perked up. "That's amazing," she said. As Dr. Duncan moved on with the tests, she burst into tears.

"I know that we still have a long way to go, but we need to stop right now and thank God for this good news," Mom said. "We haven't had any in a long time. Let's pause and thank Him for what He is doing."

Right there in the doctor's office, we did just that.

ANTHONY

Mommy stayed so strong that the times she did break down, you realized she was carrying an enormous burden of anxiety and pain. Every now and then, the burden would break loose and her emotions would spill out. It's good to be strong and of good courage, but it's okay to be human too. Jesus cried. In anguish, the Bible says in Luke 22:44, He sweat "great drops of blood" while facing the cross (KJV). That's the gospel. God became human too.

> It's good to be strong and of good courage, but it's okay to be human too.

PRISCILLA

It wasn't long before things changed and Mom's report was not so good. Another scan showed the tumors were growing.

"I'm afraid I don't have an option for you," her medical doctor told us. "Surgically, there's nothing we can do. Any action we could take would make things worse. At this point it's best to let the cancer run its course."

The doctor was incredibly kind but direct. It was devastating news to hear.

"I just want to make it to seventy years old," Mom said.

If there was ever a time to trust God and believe that the Holy Spirit would move miraculously, it was then. We needed to put away whatever concerns we had about not burdening others and ask for help and for prayer. My parents had always been careful about not overextending themselves in people's lives or taking advantage of their leadership roles. So, at this point, we hadn't even publicly disclosed the severity of Mom's condition.

But there is a time to help others and a time to let others help you. I knew I would have to communicate that to my father.

"Dad, the church has been asking what they can do to help us," I said to him. "Not only our home church but the global church, too, the body of Christ. People want to bring food. They want to pray. We are all exhausted. It's time to tell everyone what's going on."

Dad agreed. We told Bobby Gibson, one of the associate pastors at our church, about Mom's latest report, and God's people immediately jumped into action. Food began to arrive, and folks in the community showed up every day around noon to march around our parents' house and pray. Even

> There is a time to help others and a time to let others help you.

though they could not visit Mom, old friends came from far away, just to stand in the front yard and offer prayer, to be there for us in a hard time.

We would open the blinds or make a video of the prayer marches so Mom could see them, and she would watch and cry. Everything had always been focused on Dad's ministry or even us kids. But all the while it was Mom's work behind the scenes that kept the machine going. No doubt, seeing this many people praying for her and focusing on her recovery was a great encouragement.

We were all so hopeful then, believing for a miracle. I would rather err on the side of faith than discouragement. Go down believing God. Even in her condition, by example, Mom was leading us to hold on and believe.

That being said, we did not want to live in denial. For a faith person, that is hard. You don't want to avoid the important discussions, but how do you have real, honest conversations about the possibility of death and still remain in faith?

As time passed it became clear that Mom's health was declining. Prayers and blessings continued to pour in from around the world. Pastor Jim Cymbala arranged for his entire congregation, along with the Brooklyn Tabernacle Choir, to sing a song of healing for Mom. We all watched that video with tears streaming down our faces, hands lifted, saying, *Yes, Lord. Amen.*

Messages came from Kenya to the United Kingdom, from Miami to Calgary, from neighbors and strangers citywide, corporate and worldwide prayers for Mom's complete healing. The body of Christ came together to love our family and Mom, and we will never forget it as long as we live.

Mom focused on three goals: make it to the Kingdom Legacy Live event in mid-November, to her seventieth birthday on December 1, and to her fiftieth wedding anniversary in June 2020.

Kingdom Legacy was held on November 8, and Mom felt like she was able to go. We prayed that she would not only be able to attend but also enjoy this special night.

JONATHAN

We assured Mom that we would take care of everything to make the event as easy for her as possible. A coworker came to help and escort her to the church. Mom sat quietly backstage as we all loved on her and took family pictures.

> The body of Christ came together to love our family and Mom, and we will never forget it as long as we live.

As the night was set to begin, Mom waited by the steps that led from the greenroom to the sanctuary. She was on a lot of pain medication, and I could tell from the look on her face that it was going to take every ounce of energy just to navigate those stairs. But she wanted to do it by herself.

A few minutes before showtime, Anthony signaled for everyone to get in place. Mom stood, walked down the steps, and made her way to the front row, taking the seat that she had occupied every Sunday and Wednesday for the last thirty years. It was the first lady's chair, a role and responsibility that Mom took very seriously.

The congregation applauded, showing their love and appreciation, then the lights went down and the music started. I watched Mom a moment longer, struggling but poised, frail, and yet so strong.

ANTHONY

I started my own production company a few years back, so I brought in my team, and we began to organize Kingdom Legacy Live. Of all the projects I've done in Los Angeles and all the big names I've worked with, this was the most meaningful: to pay tribute to the one who made me his namesake, the man I am honored to call "Daddy."

I called in the big guns for Dad's special night. The best lighting gear and camera crews and the top producers from L.A. For performers, I reached out to Natalie Grant, Jeremy Camp, Lecrae, Kirk Franklin, Donnie McClurkin, and Tori Kelly. Everyone was quick to say yes. And Sherri Shepherd, from *The View*, signed on to host the event. These weren't simply performance contracts I sent out to people in the business; these were close friends who wanted to show their gratitude to my father for his faithful service of more than fifty years.

Oak Cliff Bible Fellowship was packed for Kingdom Legacy Live. Tori sang a song she had written about going through trials called "Before the Dawn." It poetically paints a picture of how everything beautiful comes with pain. A pain that God in His kindness redeems.

It's always darkest right before the dawn
So keep your head up

As Tori's voice soared on the second chorus, I peeked from backstage to where my parents were seated. Mommy was smiling so big. Dad holding her hand. As Tori sang about roses and thorns, I had each of Mom's grandchildren walk out and hand her a single red rose.

It was a sweet reminder to her that they loved their Nonny and to keep her head up.

At the end of the evening, Mom caught my sleeve.

"Anthony, you did an amazing job," she said. "But it was *so* long."

I wrapped my arms around her as we shared a laugh.

"I'm just glad you were here."

We all shed a few tears that night. For once, they were good tears.

PRISCILLA

I felt as if the Lord let us have that weekend together. It lifted all our spirits. Dad even did a little dance step with Kirk onstage.

During the following Sunday services, Oak Cliff celebrated Mom's and Dad's seventieth birthdays, and Mom was able to be there for that as well. It was the last time she would ever step foot inside our church.

A lot of people don't realize our Daddy's got moves!

TONY

Kingdom Legacy Live was a special night for all of us. Lois was weak but determined to celebrate our accomplishments. I was excited she could be there but hurt because she was just so ill.

ANTHONY

How could God call you to make history and at the same time take away the person who helped you get there?

TONY

That was a divine contradiction. The greatest day in the worst season.

CHRYSTAL

The rest of the year held hope-filled days on one hand, and days filled with action, on the other. Faith makes things possible, but without works, faith is also dead. We chose to live with no regrets, doing every-thing we could to use every tool at our disposal—every prayer, every treatment option, and every form of faith and belief.

I once told Daddy I wanted to sit with Mom, look through the old pictures, and reminisce about the past. I wanted to do this as a joint venture and ask her what she was thinking as we traveled through time together.

"Well, I don't understand what's stopping you from doing that," he said.

"Because I'm afraid I will communicate to her that I'm hoping for her healing but not convinced that healing will come."

I did my best to be there in each moment. I wanted to be present in both reality and hopeful expectation. The truth? I'm not sure I did so great with either one. I always felt torn between the two.

I think Mom felt that same tension. She believed God would heal her. She didn't feel as if this was her time to leave us and go to heaven. There were also times when she would dip her toes in the potential of her passing and talk about the possibility of not being around.

"Y'all need to make sure and take care of your father," she told us. "He needs to keep going. He's not old, and he's nowhere near being ready to stop. I know your daddy. If he doesn't keep preaching, he'll die."

We were all caught between expectancy and reality. We didn't want to say too much, but none of us wanted to regret the things we had left unsaid.

PRISCILLA

I wanted to ride the balance between faith and regret. It's so easy to get busy and distracted, thinking there is always more time. I wanted to talk to Mom about all those little things we experienced growing up. She was born in Guyana, South America, and would make these incredible Guyanese dishes for us. Chrystal and I wanted to cook those dishes with her again and cement our knowledge of the recipes. We wanted to hear the stories about how she learned them and what it was like in South America when she was a kid. We'd heard it all before, but we wanted to hear it again and again.

> It's so easy to get busy and distracted, thinking there is always more time.

Truth be told, I hope my children will

still want to cook these dishes for their kids so they will have a little reminder of their great-grandmother. For me, pepper pot (a traditional Guyanese dish) will always taste like home.

Even if Mom was too weak to get out of bed, she maintained a sense of hopefulness and insisted that those around her do the same. But though her hope was extravagant, she remained grounded in reality, having conversations with us that were very frank.

One day she handed Chrystal and me some paperwork and said, "Okay, I wrote everything down. Here is a picture of the casket I'd like to have and the flower arrangements that I think are beautiful. And this is a picture of Billy and Ruth Graham's burial site. I love the simplicity of it. I want a memorial just like this." Then she pointed to a necklace in her jewelry case. It was a small silver cross on a simple chain.

"Put this around my neck when you bury me."

TONY

I kept believing that God would heal Lois. But it was mixed with disappointment, particularly once we saw the traditional medical approach wasn't having any effect. I was fighting to keep strong for her, believing for healing.

JONATHAN

It seemed that during this time we were stunned again and again by devastating news. How could this have happened? What were we supposed to do now?

Mom was the one who strengthened us in that time. She kept saying to us, "You can't stop. You've got to keep going. Preach the Word. Get the gospel out there. This is spiritual warfare, Ephesians 6:12."

It took some time, but eventually I thought, *Okay, that is exactly what we're going to do.* We are going to fight, and we are going to win. If God is for us, who can be against us? We are more than conquerors in Jesus Christ. We have been chosen and redeemed. I'm going in full force. In my mind, there's nothing left to do but go hard. And so, yes, I'm staying on Philippians 4:6 all day and 1 John 5:14 all day and all night. We are going to pray and believe and come against the Enemy with everything we've got. We are going hard.

ANTHONY

Jon Jon's the athlete of the family, full-on sports guy, former fullback with the Dallas Cowboys. He's got that winner's mindset. Failure is not an option. There's not even a place for it in his brain.

PRISCILLA

All of us had high expectations about what God could do. I believe we still do. We trusted God could heal Mom, but we also had confidence in His sovereignty and love for us. And since Mom had assurance that God could heal, our confidence continued to be reinforced. But we were careful to balance expectation with reality and God's will. Keeping those two realities in constant tension was an ongoing struggle.

JONATHAN

I wanted to make sure that we took all of our brothers and sisters in Christ into battle with us, that we rallied all the troops to run in the same direction. We put it out on social media: "We need people to fast and pray with us for Mom's healing."

We prayed and we prayed and we prayed and we proclaimed victory. I said that once it was all over and Mommy was healed, we were going to drop a flag down to the ground and publicly declare what God has done. So, yes, we faced an incredible trial. But I had an incredible expectation.

God's people didn't show up for just a day or two. Every day, my mother's house was surrounded. Pastor Hawkins would march around the property proclaiming that cancer would fall like the walls of Jericho. We would see him out there walking and crying out to the Lord. He had been in ministry with Mom and Dad for thirty-five years, and even in his seventies, he was out there, marching around our home.

Pastors from other churches showed up too. Bryan Carter would pray over the house, touching the bricks, calling for healing in Jesus' name. The saints of God prayed every single day, every hour, for months on end. People all across the world were praying.

How could we not believe for victory? Surely, God had everyone's attention now. If an unrighteous judge will show favor, how much more will a righteous judge do?

We would make a trip to MD Anderson Cancer Center in Houston, fully expecting a miracle. Then we'd get knocked back down again with a bad report. As we watched Mommy decline, I prayed and pushed even harder, but I could not deny what I was seeing happen right in front of me. Mom was losing weight, losing energy. It was getting difficult for her to make the drive.

There was a huge chasm between what we were seeing and what we were believing for. And the space was growing wider every day.

SIX

SHE NEVER LOST HER SMILE

We sorrow but not as those who have no hope.

—1 THESSALONIANS 4:13

ANTHONY

My faith felt unshakable even though we kept getting bad news. We'd make the trip down to Mom's appointments in Houston, and she would say, "Be ready to sing 'Raise a Hallelujah,' Anthony, because I know this is going to be a good report!" Then the doctor would shake his head and say, "The cancer is still growing."

With each hit of bad news, Mommy would get this stoic look on her face, like, *Okay, let's wrap it up.* Yet somehow, even with one negative report after another, I felt sure she would come through and be healthy again. Eventually, it was evident that Mommy's condition was declining, and later that fall, she stopped going for treatment. It got to the point where she just wasn't feeling up to it and the medical industry's best efforts didn't seem to be working anyway.

Still, I held on to hope. I did not want anybody talking about loss around my mother. I was trying to keep our spirits high.

Some people do their best to be sensitive while others feel like they need to keep it real, but I wouldn't trade anything for those sweet moments of expectation that Mom and I shared.

PRISCILLA

One day, near the end of November 2019, I was sitting in the living room with Mom when Dad walked in after running a quick errand. He sat in his chair and stared straight ahead for a few minutes.

Finally, he said, "I think Two Daddy is in his last days. He laid down to take a nap, and the caretaker had a hard time waking him up. His body is giving out. I don't think it will be much longer."

Though we knew Two Daddy was struggling, just the week before, my family and I had made one of our regular visits to Baltimore. We'd gone out to eat, and he had devoured his favorite meal at his favorite restaurant: pancakes at the Double T Diner on Baltimore National Pike. We joked around, laughing at his hilarious commentary on life, and played some rounds of checkers. He seemed to be fine. And now, all of a sudden, we're at the end? Why now?

I saw the weight on Dad's face, looking at his wife, who was trying so hard to hang on but clearly getting weaker by the day. Then he gets the news that his father is likely in his last days.

ANTHONY

It was like watching a powerlifter attempt to pick up a massive weight. He strains and sweats and gives it all he's got. Even though he is shaking, with a great struggle, he somehow manages to get the weight up off his chest. But then, before the powerlifter can even catch his breath, another hundred pounds is stacked on the bar.

What can you do? It took everything you had to lift the weight before, and now it is even heavier!

PRISCILLA

Really, it felt that way for all of us. We were pressing in close, trying to hold up Dad, trying to help bear the burden. It was an incredibly difficult decision. Your wife is fading while your father is dying. Do you stay or go?

"Go," Mom told him. "You need to go."

My husband, Jerry, got on the plane with Dad, and I followed the next day. When we got there, Two Daddy was hanging on, but clearly the end was near. He could not open his eyes, couldn't speak, but he would try to squeeze our hands as we held on to his.

I looked down at him and prayed, *Lord, if this is Two Daddy's time, would You please take him home easily and before Dad has to go back to Dallas on Monday? Because we do have to go back, God. Mom is not doing well. So please don't make Daddy have to leave his father still breathing, hanging on to life, to go to his wife.*

I said "amen" and thought, *Dear Jesus, that is a lot to ask.*

At six o'clock Monday morning, November 25, Arthur "Two Daddy" Evans took his final breath. I was sad but grateful that God had answered my prayer. Dad was able to settle a few details with the funeral home and pick out the suit for his father's burial. We took out Two Daddy's Bible and read a few Scriptures he had underlined. Then Dad closed Two Daddy's well-loved, worn Bible, put it in his bag, and we flew back home.

ANTHONY

The whole family packed up to fly to my grandfather's house for his funeral. I was about to board the plane. I loved Two Daddy with all my heart, but I knew I was supposed to stay behind.

"Sorry, I can't do it," I told them. "I'm not leaving Mommy here alone."

Mom has always been the strong one, always the one to sacrifice her well-being for the family. I knew she would never in a million years ask anyone to stay. When she knew I was staying behind, she cried and said, "Baby, I'm never going to forget this."

I lay in my parents' bed and held my mom's hand. All through the night I slept right where Dad would have slept, praying harder than I had ever prayed in my life. I was still so hopeful that God was going to heal my mom.

PRISCILLA

Dad's not much of an event planner, much less a funeral planner, so Chrystal and I did our best, with Jonathan's help, to make the arrangements. The day before Two Daddy's memorial service, we all returned to Maryland to clean out the old family home we had grown up visiting as children. Our grandparents had lived in the same house for sixty years. My father grew up there. Every one of us had childhood memories in that house. Uncle Bo was gone. Aunt Beverly too. Now Two Daddy. It felt like an entire chapter of our lives was coming to a close.

We carefully removed the stained glass from over the front door and wrapped Two Mama's silver flatware and china plates. We gathered up her iron skillets, rolling pins, photo albums, and keepsakes. We put a sign on the old piano to let the moving company know that we wanted it to come to Dallas too. There were so many memories from our childhoods and my father's childhood. We used the few hours we had to gather keepsakes that could help ensure the Evans' legacy continued with our children and our children's children.

Then we took a deep breath and said goodbye to our grandparents' home.

My lung surgery was scheduled for the same week as Two Daddy's funeral. I called the surgeon and told him what was going on.

"Is there any way I can delay this for one more month without putting myself in jeopardy?"

He said that whatever it was in my chest was slow growing. So, yes, for now, we could wait—but not long.

When December 1 came, Mom turned seventy. It was the day she had asked the Lord to let her see. One of her closest friends, Rhoda, had celebrated with a tea party at her home earlier in November. The women in our family had gathered in our fanciest pajamas and hats while eating scones and sipping tea. Rhoda's son plays the harp, so he serenaded us with beautiful, calming music while we sipped. Mom loved a good tea party.

Then our entire family gathered at my house for a huge celebration with balloons and decorations everywhere. All her grandchildren and great-grandchildren had written out a special message to read, and one by one, all sixteen of them did just that.

Mommy fought hard and never lost her smile.

CHRYSTAL

"Was I awake the whole time?" Mom asked me on the ride home. She was on Dilaudid for pain by that point, and from what we could gather by watching her, that medication can make you pretty fuzzy.

"Yeah, Mommy," I replied. "You did really great."

She smiled and shook her head. After a while, she said, "I just pray I make it to Christmas."

My mother loved Christmas. The music, the candles, the trees. Yes, *trees*. She always had multiple Christmas trees. Lord, she loved to decorate. Mommy was Mrs. Claus in the flesh. Every year during the holidays, our childhood home looked like Santa Claus threw up all over our house inside and out!

By the time Christmas Day came that year, Mom was in and out. Her need for pain meds had increased, so I'm sure that was the reason why. Now that I think back, it could have also been that she was simply exhausted from the fight.

She slept.

A *lot*.

But Christmas morning, I brought her a gift, a custom-made circular wooden ornament with her name carved inside. I walked from the back door and through the living room. The lights on the tree were twinkling, and "O Holy Night" was playing from a disc that had been in the CD player since the Christmas before.

As I entered her dimly lit bedroom, I called her name. She laid still. I called her name again as I moved closer to her. She stirred. When I was within reach, I laid my hand on her arm and said, "Merry Christmas, Mommy."

She opened her eyes.

I smiled and held up her ornament. She smiled back.

"You made it, Mommy," I said. "Thank you for staying with me for one more Christmas Day."

She cleared her throat and reached for the ornament to examine it up close. "Merry Christmas, Chrystal," she said. "I love it."

TONY

Lois heard voices telling her there were only a few days left, and one time she saw her mom and dad. "Don't you see them?" she asked. I wish the Lord would have let me see them, too, but I'm glad she was able to be comforted in that moment.

I thought about chapter 7 of Acts. Stephen was about to be stoned to death by the Sanhedrin. Filled with the Spirit, he saw the heavens open and Jesus standing at the Father's right hand. Sometimes God lets faithful believers see where they're headed. That makes the transition easier.

Death by stoning is truly a hard way to go. But the Bible says that after Stephen forgave his assailants, he fell asleep. That's how the Lord views dying. It's only sleep.

ANTHONY

I watched my mom's health fade to the point that it was hard to keep believing for something good. Not that I doubted God, but it felt almost selfish. She was suffering so much physically that I just wanted her to be well. Faith is our legacy. The ultimate health is to live forever with God.

After Christmas, Mom was in immense pain, and the medication wasn't having much effect. Her breathing had changed, gotten slower.

> **Faith is our legacy. The ultimate health is to live forever with God.**

TONY

Our family friend, Dr. Stewart, stopped by on December 29 to bring us food. I told him Lois was pretty weak. He had his stethoscope in the car, so he came in and checked Mom's breathing.

His diagnosis was compassionate but clear. "Her lungs are filling up," he said sadly. "It probably won't be much longer now."

My four children and I gathered together. I was lying beside Lois, rubbing her arm when I dozed off.

Chrystal woke me. "Dad, I think it's getting close to time."

There were longer gaps between her breathing, so I got up and read Psalm 91:2–6 over her.

> I will say concerning the LORD, who is my refuge and
>   my fortress,
> my God in whom I trust:
> He himself will rescue you from the bird trap,
> from the destructive plague.
> He will cover you with his feathers;
> you will take refuge under his wings.
> His faithfulness will be a protective shield.
> You will not fear the terror of the night,
> the arrow that flies by day,
> the plague that stalks in darkness,
> or the pestilence that ravages at noon.

A tear streamed down her cheek. I watched my wife of fifty years fade from earth, grateful that our children were there to share the moment. I prayed, *Lord, if this is Your will, then I am going to yield to Your will.*

Anthony sang, and we all cried many tears. We told her how thankful we were for giving us so much, for all her sacrifice and love.

ANTHONY

"Fighting for Us" is one of my mom's favorite songs, so I leaned in close, singing in her ear:

You won't hold back when it comes to Your children
You're fighting for us

"I love you, Mommy," I whispered when the song was done. We listened to more worship music, some of mine, some from friends, other songs that she loved. We thanked her for all the sacrifices over the years, for the investment she had made day in and day out in our lives.

We said goodbye. Because that is what the Lord chose in that moment. Great expectations met with great disappointment. You are never ready to lose a parent. There is no way to prepare.

It was the hardest thing I have ever had to do.

JONATHAN

We begged God for a yes. It felt like the whole world was pleading. But God said no.

TONY

Lois and I met when we were eighteen. We were just kids. She became my wife, my lover, my prayer partner, my biggest defender. Lois was my best friend.

But near the end, she said, "Tony, let me go."

> We begged God for a yes. It felt like the whole world was pleading. But God said no.

ANTHONY

The night my mother passed away I had to board a plane to perform at a New Year's Eve event in London. When I saw Big Ben from the airplane window, I was smiling with tears in my eyes. Mom loved London. And she was insistent that God's work keep moving on.

"Well, Mommy," I said as the jet touched down at Heathrow. "Here I am."

I stood on that stage, feeling so many things. Before I began to sing, I shared the story of my mother's passing the night before and how she had made us all promise that our ministering would not stop.

The crowd stood and applauded. They were not clapping for me but for the legacy of Lois Evans—the woman who made sure we kept the gospel going. It wasn't about being onstage or singing a great worship song or any of those things. It was about God showing up in the moment. Even in disappointment, even when your life has been torn to shreds. Even when you are heartbroken and feel like you cannot continue. God's work moves on. Beyond my mother or father or me or my siblings, beyond grandkids or great-grandkids to the tenth generation, the Lord's purpose prevails.

Call me crazy or grief-stricken, but I promise, in that moment, Mom was right there with me in the city she so loved, clapping along with us, excited that her Kingdom Legacy was moving ahead.

Anthony, she whispered to me with a smile. *I am fine.*

Lois Irene Evans, beloved wife of Tony Evans for forty-nine years, and founder of Pastors' Wives Ministry, passed away December 30, 2019, of biliary cancer. She was seventy.

Tony, senior pastor of Oak Cliff Bible Fellowship in Dallas, shared the news on Facebook. "Just before the sun came up this morning," he wrote, "the love of my life transitioned from earth and watched her first sunrise from heaven.

"As she slipped away, we told her how much we love her, how proud we are of her, and how thankful we are for the life she has lived," Pastor Evans wrote. "We are what we are because of her."

Priscilla Shirer, bestselling author, actress, and the Evans' daughter, tweeted, "Goodnight, my beautiful, beloved Mommy. I'll see you in the morning."

The Evans' son, Christian music artist Anthony Evans, Jr., posted, "I love you forever, Mommy."

SEVEN

STONES OF REMEMBRANCE

This hope we have as an anchor of the soul, both sure and steadfast, and which enters the Presence behind the veil.

—HEBREWS 6:19 NKJV

PRISCILLA

Mom's celebration service was held January 6 at Oak Cliff Bible Fellowship. Thousands attended, so it was like planning a major event. We wanted to honor her as best we could, but planning a service for so many people required a great deal of time and energy. In hindsight, I realize that we robbed ourselves of the time and space to grieve, but honestly, I'd do it all over again. It was amazing!

ANTHONY

Pastor Gibson began with these words: "This is *still* the day that the Lord has made. And we will rejoice and be glad in it. We all know our first lady didn't want a dull service in any sort of way. So we are here to celebrate life and a life well lived."

We called Mom's service "A Celebration of Life and Legacy." I sang one of Mommy's favorites, and Kirk Franklin helped with the music for the entire memorial. God bless Kirk. He's family, like another brother to me and a son to Mommy and Daddy. In fact, Kirk always called my mother "Mama Lo."

JONATHAN

I gave the eulogy. All of us did, really. You never think you would be able to preach your own mother's funeral, but I knew it was something that would make her heart glad and honor her service and sacrifice in our lives. It would help me as well. When God speaks through us, He speaks to us.

I am not going to tell you that it was easy, but it was good. God's people packed the pews at Oak Cliff to pay tribute to my mom. She impacted every person there in some way, brothers and sisters and spiritual sons and daughters.

I stepped into my father's pulpit as he watched from the front row. I felt weak yet strong, honored, heartbroken, and overwhelmed. But somehow I also felt encouraged.

I looked over to where Dad was seated.

"I want to thank you for being a good husband and a good father," I said. "I saw the way you treated Mommy and your level of patience, understanding, discernment, and wisdom. You helped me become a better husband. When I think about how I need to grow, I simply ask myself, *What did Daddy do?* And that's what I try to do."

Then I called my siblings to join me on the platform.

"Chrystal is Mommy's light," I said. "She's the first child. She brought light. She made Mom and Dad a family. Priscilla is Mommy's honor. She lives to honor, respect, and be a blessing for her mother.

Anthony is priceless because he has the ability to connect to Mom's heart." I paused for dramatic effect. "And, well, *I* am the favorite."

Everybody laughed at that, from the first pew to the rafters. I imagine Mommy was laughing too. (Because she knows it's true.)

"What gives me hope are the words my mother shared with us in her final days," I continued. "One night I was standing by her bedside, and she said, 'Yes, sir.' She was fading in and out of consciousness. 'Yes, sir,' she said again. 'Days? Two days? Whatever. Just take me up.'

"Another time, she looked at me and asked, 'Mommy? Did you see Mommy?' Mom called her mother Mommy too.

"'No, ma'am,' I replied. 'I didn't see her.'

"'My mother,' she said. 'She was just sitting right here. You didn't see her?'

"'I didn't see her,' I said, 'but I'm glad you did.'

"Near the very end, she was sleeping in her wheelchair and suddenly opened her eyes. 'Praise God!' she said.

"It's painful to watch your mother become so fragile and slip away, but I knew in that moment she was in the presence of the Lord. 'Oh, it's real,' I replied."

Priscilla came up next and told the crowd her story about Mom's final days.

PRISCILLA

Mom opened her eyes in a little bit of consciousness and said, "They're trying to give me an award. There's an award. But they can't find the right song."

Mom repeated that several times over the course of two or three days at the beginning of December. We took note but didn't think much of it until a few days before her death. Dad and I were with her in the bedroom and turned on a playlist of worship songs. By chance, the first melody to fill the air was "Victory Belongs to Jesus" by Todd Dulaney. As soon as Mom heard it, her eyes shot open, and she sat nearly straight up in the bed.

"That's it," she said with hope in her eyes. "That's the song."

Hold on, the song tells us. Hold on. The victory belongs to Jesus. That's all any of us could do. Pray and hold on.

Despite her pain, Mom still led us in worship.

JONATHAN

The whole congregation stood and sang "Victory Belongs to Jesus" while the big screens scrolled through pictures from Mom's life. The song inspired my message that morning. So with every eye on me, I began to preach.

First Corinthians 15:57 says that even in this day, we can still be thankful to God who has given us victory in Jesus. I know that my mother was foreknown and predestined to be conformed into the image of the Son because we have victory in Christ Jesus. If God is for you, not even death can be against you because we have victory in Jesus. In this world we will have loss and trouble, but we have victory in Christ because Christ has already overcome the world.

We are suffering, but not crushed. I am perplexed, but I will not be driven to despair. I am strengthened by His loving hand. All things work together for good, for those who love God and are called according to His purpose, because we have victory in Jesus Christ. The only reason I can get up here and have the strength to speak God's Word is because God's Word is speaking to me. Even in distress, we still have victory in Jesus.

That doesn't mean that I do not wrestle with God. If we have victory in Your name, didn't You hear us when we were praying? Didn't You see the people walking around my parents' house? Did You hear the prayers of Bishop T. D. Jakes and Bryan Carter, Jim Cymbala, Antioch and Friendship-West, Gateway and The Village, churches around the world both big and small?

Where are You, Lord? Didn't You hear us calling? Why didn't You do what we asked? Your Word says that if we abide in You and Your Word abides in us, then we can ask whatever we desire, and it will be given to us. Your Word tells us that if we ask according to Your will, that You hear us. Mark 11 says, if we pray believing, we *will* receive. Philippians 4 says be anxious for nothing, but in all things, by prayer and supplication, to make our requests known.

So my question, God, is, *Where are You? This was an opportunity for us to see Your glory!*

And as I was wrestling with the Lord, He answered me.

"You don't understand the nature of my victory," God said. "Just because I didn't answer your prayer in your way doesn't mean that I haven't already answered your prayer anyway. Victory already belonged to your mother. There were always only two answers to your prayers. Either she was going to be healed or she was going to be *Healed*. Either she was going to live or she was going to *Live*. She was either going to be with family or she was *Going to Be with Family*. Victory was assured regardless. The two answers to your prayer were always yes and *Yes*. Because victory belongs to Christ Jesus.

"I am the sovereign God, and my game plan is far bigger than any one player on the field. So, trust in Me with all of your heart and lean not on your own understanding. Lean on Me because only I have the ability to make a crooked situation straight. As high as the heavens are above the earth, so are My ways higher than yours, and My thoughts above than your thoughts. I appreciate your prayers and trust, but I am God. Don't tell Me how to get My glory. Don't come to Me with entitlement. Without My victory, all of you would be on the doorsteps of hell.

"I know it was hard for you to watch your mother die. But I watched My Son die so that your mother could live. My grace is sufficient for you."

What could I say? *The Lord gives. The Lord takes. Thanks be to God.*

Dad taught me this simple verse when I was a kid. Acts 13:36. David served the purposes of God for the benefit of a generation. And then he fell asleep. There is no better summary of a successful life. Lois Evans served the purposes of God for her generation. And then she fell asleep.

So I have been able to step back and reflect on the fact that Mom was a great player on God's team. When I was playing football, my coach would always say, "Remember what's coming. Play in light of what's coming."

In the NFL, every player takes the field on Sunday, but really, they are thinking about Monday. You know why? Monday is when you review the film of your performance. Monday is accountability day. The head coach would pull down the screen, pick up his red pointer, and ask this question: "Did you play for the team? Did you honor that logo on your helmet? Did you follow the playbook that you were given? Or were you just out there doing your own thing? Don't answer. We're about to find out, right now."

One day the game will be over, and our coach, God the Father, will want to know, "Did you live your life based upon My playbook? Were you playing for the coach or the crowd? Did you honor the King of kings' logo? Or were you just out there doing your own thing?"

My mom would want me to let you know that if you cannot answer those questions, then you need to make a change. Because every person wants to hear what my mom has already heard. "Well done, My good and faithful servant. Well done."

> **There is no better summary of a successful life. Lois Evans served the purposes of God for her generation. And then she fell asleep.**

Joshua chapter 4 talks about the stones of remembrance. He gave them to twelve men to keep in their homes so that any time their children asked about the stones, they would have an opportunity to tell the stories of God's provision, every step of the way.

Our family—the Evanses, the Hursts, the Shirers—we have stones of remembrance. We gave Mom and Dad a set of these stones, each inscribed with a virtue of belief, values they instilled in each of us, the principles we pass down to our children and that we pray will continue to roll on through every generation until Jesus returns to take us all home.

These stones were placed near Mom's casket. I asked my siblings to choose one and testify to the impact it had in their lives.

Then one by one my siblings came back to the podium to share about the stone they had selected.

CHRYSTAL

Since I'm the oldest, I was the first to speak.
I picked up a stone with the word *legacy*.

Every Christmas Mom could be found in her kitchen, cooking like crazy. This year Mom was still with us, but she was obviously not going to be preparing the meal. As we talked about the menu, her menu, it became clear that over the years Mommy had shown each of us how to make one or two of her famous dishes, passing on her own special "twist of the wrist." Even though she wasn't able to do the cooking, Christmas dinner still got done. Mommy had shared her knowledge, skill, and gift of gracious hospitality, building her legacy one lesson at a time. That's how legacy is built, you know. One small moment at a time. Doing the right thing, for the right reasons, for an impact that lasts long after you are gone.

Mom loved to watch the sunset. More than a few times we'd be driving home and have to pull over to catch the view of an orange sun sinking in that big Texas sky. She would always express awe, sharing her excitement in audible ways. Her oohs and aahs would cease only long enough for her to pull out her phone, lean out the window, and take some pictures. And then, of course, she'd edit them to put on Instagram so she could admire the sunsets long after that day had passed.

One of our favorite places to watch the sunset was Lake Palestine in Tyler, Texas. It was a wonder to behold the water rippling against the brilliant colors radiating off the setting sun.

The ripples of my mother's life are beautiful to behold too. But ripples don't happen on their own. They start with something. A wisp of wind can propel tiny waves across the water. One small pebble tossed into a still pond can too. Ripples provide proof of the pebble's impact. It doesn't matter that the pebble is small. Its presence still has power. The evidence that it has pierced the water lasts long after the impact has occurred.

This is how we build legacy, one small and sometimes seemingly insignificant action or decision at a time that ripples long after the initial impact. Just like I can see the ripples on the water during a sunset and not know where they began, I believe that people will see the legacy of my mother's life for many years and not even realize where the impact began.

Mommy built her legacy because she was willing to pick up the tiniest, most insignificant pebbles. Before she was the executive vice president of the Urban Alternative, the national ministry for our father, Mom was Oak Cliff Bible Fellowship's first secretary, first choir director, first children's leader. She would type up our church programs and copy and fold them by hand. And for every event and gathering she would cook or prepare some kind of treat. As the firstborn, I got to see her faithfulness in the seemingly small things, day in and day out. She was willing to be unseen and often was not celebrated. But Mom trusted that God saw it all. She believed that He would take her little and make much, far beyond what she could see. In His kingdom, there are no small things. I witnessed legacy being created firsthand. Mom's legacy has rippled far beyond the borders of our home and local church.

> **This is how we build legacy, one small and sometimes seemingly insignificant action or decision at a time that ripples long after the initial impact.**

Mom taught me to care. I have a friend who is a missionary in the Dominican Republic. She became weary in the work and wanted to come home. But Mom got on the phone and encouraged her to hang in and stay faithful to the call. Because my friend stayed, many girls have been rescued from sex trafficking. Because many were rescued, many babies have been born. All because my mother took the time to reach out and listen to this one woman. One small pebble, and its ripples will impact generations to come.

Mom taught me to listen. She always stayed after church until everyone who wanted to talk with her had done so. And she listened until they had said everything they needed to say. There are many gifted speakers in ministry, but Mom also had the gift of listening. She listened to us not only with her ears but with her eyes and her heart as well. Mom saw me. She saw through me. And she accepted and celebrated me for who I am. Her listening ear was a gift, and she gave that gift to thousands over the years. Many know God's love because He loved them through a woman named Lois.

Mom taught me to sacrifice. I was a single college student when my first baby was born. Mommy came and stayed with me for three weeks. We slept in the same bed. She would hold tiny Kariss during the night so I could catch a few minutes of rest. When the time of her caring for me and my new baby girl was over, I drove her to the Greyhound bus station. It was a cold, bitter day in November, and while we were standing there waiting, I saw her for the first time. She was my mom but not *just* my mom. She was a woman with her own hopes and dreams. A woman who had given up so much to come and help me in that season of my life, even though I had made a mess of things. In that moment, so much was clear. I could see her, and I was able to feel the size of her sacrifice.

When the bus pulled in to take her away, I threw my arms around her and started bawling. I couldn't bear the thought of being apart. "Don't cry," Mommy said. "I'll see you shortly. You'll be coming home soon."

God gave us a picture of things to come. Even now, in grief, I think of that day and hear her reminding me, *Don't cry. I will see you again soon.*

Mom taught me that impact is important. Her commitment to the Lord and her understanding of legacy was evident in the way she chose to live her life. Tony Evans always brought the Word, but Lois Evans brought the wonder. And because of that, we are blessed by her legacy. The ripples continue to this day and for many days to come.

I loved being firstborn!

I was overwhelmed and a bit shaky when I returned to my seat. Not because I was nervous—I've spent many years speaking in front of large crowds—but because of the impact my remembrances had brought to me regarding my mother's influence over every facet of my life.

PRISCILLA

Chrystal nodded and passed me the microphone. I turned the stone in my hand before I began to speak.

The stone I chose was *faith.*

About six weeks ago, Mom was lying in bed, scrolling through Facebook. Several of us were in the room. All of a sudden, she burst into tears.

"Mom, what's wrong?" we asked, rushing to her side. "Why are you crying?"

She replied, "Because I see all these prayers from people in our church, from different denominations, people from different races and backgrounds and continents and countries that are praying for me and asking God to heal me. What will happen to their faith if God doesn't answer the way they're praying?"

Mom cried not for herself but for the people of God. She worried that others might waver in their faith and no longer believe that God is who He says He is and that He can still do everything that He says He can do. So if there is one thing you can do to honor my mother, it is this: Do not let your hearts be troubled. Believe that the God of Ephesians 3:20–21 is still who He says He is: Now unto Him, who is able to do exceedingly, abundantly, above and beyond anything that you can ask or think. To Him, be the glory both now and forever more in Jesus' name. Amen.

> **If there is one thing you can do to honor my mother, it is this: Do not let your hearts be troubled. Believe that the God of Ephesians 3:20–21 is still who He says He is.**

Mommy's love runs deeper than words.

There was no doubt that my mom had lived out her faith for all to see. But she always took it a step further. She prayed that everyone she came in contact with would also fully embrace, with unwavering faith and trust, the God who loved and cared for them.

ANTHONY

Speaking at your mother's funeral is not something you ever dream you'll be able to do. But there was a peace that day. I felt it. We all did. I was even able to smile.

My stone said *family*.

Mommy was a master at orchestrating family moments and memories. I thought everybody experienced that, but as I grew up, I began to understand how blessed we truly were. I didn't realize how hard she was working behind the scenes to make those moments happen so we could appreciate family time together.

We all came here today in some type of vehicle. A very important part of that vehicle is the shock absorber. It bears the impact of the road. That is what my mom has been for all of us. She absorbed the impact of what full-time ministry can do to a family, the ways it can exhaust and tear you apart. Mom got between us and the potholes of life. She was our protector and our shield.

I wish I'd have recognized earlier in life how much stress that puts on a person, to be in the middle like that. But we did eventually realize it, and I am thankful that in the last few years I was able to let her know how much I appreciated her standing in the gap, taking care of all of us, the sacrifices she made. She established a desire for family in us and memories as a family that we will hold forever in our hearts and carry on.

It was hard to not get emotional talking about Mommy. But I believe she was proud of the way we handled ourselves that day. "Stay strong," she told us. "Live out the purposes of God."

Mom's youngest was last to speak. I stepped back as he walked to center stage.

JONATHAN

I held the cool, smooth stone in my hands, looking out over the people. Deep breath. Time to bring it home.

My stone was *salvation*.

When I was six years old, Mom led me to Christ. One thing she would want me to be sure and communicate to you this morning is the importance of salvation. We need to live out our faith and tell others about Jesus, because that is our impact and legacy. That faith is what brings us into the family of God.

Jesus Christ came into the world and lived a perfect life because you and I cannot. He is the propitiation of our sins. He satisfied God's requirement of perfection, because we don't have the ability.

For all those who place their faith in Him, He offers perfect credit to an imperfect credit score. He will raise the standard of God in you so that God can accept you, but not because of who you are, but rather because of who He is and what He has done. Death belongs to you and me, yet though Christ was blameless, He took it upon Himself.

Jesus canceled your debt by acquiring it Himself. He lived, He died, and He now forever lives so that you can live. He didn't give

His life so that you and I can go our own way. He died because *He* is the way, the truth, and the life.

And so I offer to you the same salvation my mother offered to me as a child. I want to thank my parents for not only teaching us about the Lord but showing us Christian living through their example. We will always remember the stones.

With that, Pastor Gibson came to close Mom's service. It ended the way every Evans family service ends—with the call to follow God wherever He may lead.

Jesus canceled your debt by acquiring it Himself. He lived, He died, and He now forever lives so that you can live.

TONY

Mom's greatest joy was teaching us to love Jesus.

My dear wife, Lois, loved her family more than life itself. One time in an interview I heard her say, "Our four kids were my church. With that in mind, I had to refocus on my ministry. I had been given four very special projects that would have to be seen through to completion. Someone had to instill godly principals in my children's lives, and the Lord let me know that I was the woman for the job."

EIGHT

TOMORROW HAS BEEN CANCELED

> Do not be afraid. Stand firm and you will see the
> deliverance the LORD will bring you today. The
> Egyptians you see today you will never see again.
> The LORD will fight for you; you need only to be still.
> —EXODUS 14:13–14 NIV

PRISCILLA

When someone you love passes on, it feels like the world stops. But it doesn't. The world keeps turning. My lung surgery was scheduled for the week after Mom went to heaven. With the emotional and physical exhaustion of all that had happened in the days before, I wasn't prepared to handle the upcoming operation.

> When someone you love passes on, it feels like the world stops. But it doesn't. The world keeps turning.

I called the surgeon. "Can we possibly push this back to February?" I asked. "I just buried my mom."

He brought me in for another scan later that afternoon and called early the next morning.

"Whatever is in your lung is growing," he said. "We cannot wait. We have to take it out now."

One week to the day after Mom's funeral, the surgeon removed the upper lobe of my left lung.

ANTHONY

Here we were in the same hospital, same hospital gown, one floor away from where Mommy had been, and Priscilla was having major surgery. We were all gathered in the waiting room. Time crawls in a hospital waiting room, and we had been in so many of them the last couple of years.

It slowly began to dawn on us that Silla's surgery was taking too long. They said they would keep us posted on her progress, but hours had passed without an update.

CHRYSTAL

It's just—you can't imagine the anxiety. Not at that point. We were worn out six months before Priscilla's surgery. We were beyond exhausted emotionally and physically and, yeah, spiritually too.

Eventually we heard that Priscilla had made it through the surgery. But the waiting was excruciating.

PRISCILLA

I was in the hospital for five days, and I was emotionally and physically wrecked. I had a twelve-inch drainage tube in my chest, and it was extremely painful. At one point, the nurses offered Dilaudid—a morphine variant—to help ease the pain.

I reacted immediately. "Oh no! Uh-uh!" I replied. "Not Dilaudid!"

During the last weeks of Mom's life, this was the medication we'd been carefully administering to help ease her pain. I didn't want to take it. It reminded me of the trauma we had just gone through with her. But then the pain got worse, and despite my hesitation, I changed my mind.

The powerful medication eased my pain, but it also put me into deep bouts of unconsciousness. During those hours, I could still hear everyone in the room and feel as though I was a part of whatever conversation was going on. When they laughed, I thought I was laughing with them. When they spoke, I thought I was part of the discussion. I knew where every person was sitting and what they were saying. At one point, Anthony grabbed my left hand, and although I didn't respond physically, I felt the warmth, and it tethered me to everyone in the room. I thought that I was squeezing his hand right back. I was with them.

When I fully woke from my stupor, I was so eager to tell my beloved family what I had experienced. Even though it seemed like I was out of it, I'd been a part of everything that was happening around me.

"I was right here with all of you, the entire time," I told them. "And if I felt engaged like that, it probably means that Mommy was too. She was with us even when it seemed like she wasn't. She heard us, felt the warmth of our presence, and knew that we were near."

This connection to Mom's experience was a small grace, but in that moment, tiny bits of grace were like rain in the desert to all of us.

JONATHAN

In the middle of all our pain, God let us know that Mom had heard us. She knew when we were holding her hand or rubbing her arms, when the grandkids and great-grandkids came to visit, when we laughed or cried or praised the Lord. Mom knew.

PRISCILLA

Four days after the surgery, the doctors came in with the pathology report. The growth in my lung wasn't an innocuous nodule. It was cancer. Thankfully, it hadn't spread outside of my lungs, so the surgery was curative. I would need no further treatment!

As Jerry and I drove away from the hospital the following day, we passed the oncology wing across the street. It was the same place we'd spent so many hours with Mom whenever she received radiation or chemotherapy.

"We are so blessed," I told Jerry. "We could be driving across the street to schedule chemo. Instead, we get to drive home."

Jerry squeezed my hand. "It's gonna be okay."

TONY

It knocked the wind out of me to hear that the growth in Priscilla's lung was cancer. But we had to go into action. What did we need to do? What was next?

Gratefully, for her, all that was next was recovery from this difficult and invasive surgery. Even though we had just experienced a great loss, Priscilla was still here, and we were incredibly aware in that reality of God's graciousness to us. An adenoid carcinoma in the lung is such a deadly cancer. Usually, there are no symptoms until it has already spread outside of the lung. By then, it is often too late. Priscilla's doctors continued to note the improbability of finding this cancer so early.

It was a miracle. And we needed one.

PRISCILLA

For the past two years I had been in action mode. With our fast-paced lives combined with all the fires we had to put out, there had been no time to process everything. The screeching halt of my recovery gave me some time to do that. So many family members were gone now, and I hadn't had a chance to grieve any of them.

That's the way life is sometimes, right? We start moving too fast to think straight, take care of ourselves, or recover from life's difficulties. We are resilient, putting our hands to whatever task is next and continuing to move forward. Usually that's my mode of function too. But listen, having part of your lung removed will force you to stop because you have to literally catch your breath.

> That's the way life is sometimes, right? We start moving too fast to think straight, take care of ourselves, or recover from life's difficulties.

For the next two months my calendar was cleared. No conferences. No preaching. No events. No films. No podcasts. And, praise God, for the first time in a very long time, no funerals.

When March 2020 came, I was beginning to feel a little better. I started to think about getting back to my itinerant ministry with a prescheduled event called Going Beyond Live at Overlake Christian Church in Seattle, with Anthony leading worship.

It was not to be.

Seattle was one of the initial hotbeds of the COVID-19 pandemic. At that point, no one really knew what was going on or what to expect. There was so much conflicting information in the news. Unsure of what to do, I called my doctor for advice.

"Dr. Diane, there are seven thousand people scheduled to show up at our gathering in Seattle," I began. "I have never canceled an event and wouldn't want to if it's not absolutely necessary. We don't even know what this virus thing is yet, but a real concern seems to be mounting in the Northwest. What should I do?"

Her response was measured, thoughtful, and wise: "Who will bear the brunt of responsibility if it's canceled? Is it all on you or someone else?"

I thought for a moment. "Well, our partners at Lifeway will have to take the calls of frustrated registrants. They'll have to refund fees and incur losses for finances already paid."

"Then, instead of canceling," she said, "let's just pray for the Lord to intervene if you, or the people who have registered for this event, don't need to be there for safety reasons."

Together, Jerry and I prayed that prayer. The next day Lifeway called us to say the host church had canceled the event due to a directive from the city that prohibited large gatherings. And like a row of dominoes, every other event that had been scheduled on our calendar for the rest of the year went away.

As you know, the pandemic's effect was debilitating, deadly, and widespread. Fear began to run rampant, grocery stores emptied, people struggled to breathe in ICUs while loved ones lingered in hospital parking lots because they weren't able to be by their sides in the worst of times. Millions lost their jobs, mile-long lines formed at food banks, mothers tried to figure out how to feed their children.

Never in my life had I seen such events unfold. Never in my father's life. I don't know that Two Daddy had ever witnessed anything like this pandemic in his lifetime. One by one, the lights went out until it seemed as if the entire world was in the dark.

There was, however, one thought that gave me consolation. Mommy, Two Daddy, Wynter—all the loved ones we had lost over the last two years—were in a place where there is no hunger, no sickness, no struggle, no fear. None. They were safe. They were home.

JONATHAN

The pandemic lockdown felt like another curveball thrown at our family during an already difficult time. But the whole world was hurting. And for those in ministry, that's when we go into action at a higher level. When the world shuts down, the church jumps into action.

But how can you do outreach during a quarantine? How do you lift up and help those who are suffering when human contact is a dangerous thing in itself? Mom had been sure to remind us to keep our ministries going, no matter what came against us. So we had to wade into the storm and figure out a new way of doing church.

Looking back, I don't think I had time to properly grieve. Sometimes in ministry, you don't realize you're pouring from an empty cup. There's a balance in rest and action that I don't think I had fully grasped before. Quarantine showed me that if you don't learn to slow down and refill your cup, you will end up empty.

It was difficult. It's still difficult.

> **Quarantine showed me that if you don't learn to slow down and refill your cup, you will end up empty.**

ANTHONY

Our lives were moving at a hundred miles an hour all the time and in every different direction. But then the pandemic hit, and the world felt like the Hoover Dam when they shut down the gates. Everything stops. There's no more flow. The river's not raging anymore. Stores and restaurants closed. Churches shut down. Flights were canceled. We could not do anything but sit still. We were forced to do what the Bible says in Psalm 46:10: "Be still, and know that I am God" (NIV).

As terrible as a nationwide lockdown might be, it can also work for our good. Our family had been through an extremely tough year. We needed a lot of recovery. Like an athlete, you do not recover in motion. You recover by being still.

CHRYSTAL

The new year kicked off in a crazy-busy way for us. First on the list of things to do in 2020? Bury our mother. I remember standing on the stage at Mommy's funeral, knowing I needed to stay composed. Afterward, people said, "We can't believe y'all were able to hold it together and get through that with such grace."

There was solace in having something to do. And that to-do list continued long after the graveside service. Phone calls, insurance, bank accounts, and all the documentation that must be dealt with in a very dark season. You cannot imagine how much paperwork is required after a loved one passes away. Or maybe you can.

We went straight from caring for our mother for most of 2019 to her transition from earth on the cusp of 2020, then right into all of the suspense and drama of Silla's surgery. I don't think we gave adequate credence to the number of consecutive dramas we had gone through or the deep concern about what shoe might drop next. Little did we know that shoe wouldn't be just our shoe; it would be the shoes belonging to all God's children because of a worldwide health crisis. And that crisis would shut down the entire planet.

PRISCILLA

Jerry and I parent three teenage sons, and suddenly their busy athletic lives were shut down. We weren't racing all over town to practices and sporting events. We were homeschooling again and able to be together for long stretches of time. Neither Jerry nor I were packing to head to the airport or preparing for work or ministry events.

Life as we knew it had been canceled. I was home. Gladly! My husband was home. Gladly! My children were home. Gladly! My brothers and sister were home. Daddy was home. We were all together, and we had all the time in the world. Without minimizing the tragedy of the virus and the pandemic it created, for our family, at least for the moment, the forced downtime helped us to recalibrate from the personal crises we'd faced leading up to it. So instead of complaining about it, we engaged in it and maximized this opportunity to take care of each other while still continuing moderate levels of ministry.

Among many lessons I learned in 2020, the pandemic reminded me how unnecessary we really are in the grand scheme of things. The earth keeps turning. God's work continues whether we show up at a conference or not. Isaiah 30:15 says that in returning and resting we shall be saved. Our strength lies in quiet trust.

In a sense, the Lord was leading us to still waters. Slowing down and processing the last two years of trauma was a gift. He forced us to function at a different level of trust.

ANTHONY

Like everyone else, I didn't realize the lockdown would go on for so long. At first, I looked at it like a vacation. I thought we'd be down a few weeks and then bounce back to the fast-paced world of airports and tour dates. Could anyone have imagined that movie theaters and concert halls would be empty for so long? My livelihood is travel and events, but I also believe in looking for the hopeful side of things. I wanted to use the pandemic situation as a time to learn, grow, and change.

TONY

I believe the disruption we were facing was divine. God was allowing this to interrupt the natural order of things for a divine reset, for some sovereign purpose. Something this big does not just hit the world randomly or without generational and spiritual impact. Everything changed overnight, and nobody had answers. Everybody was grappling with this unknown virus that was affecting and infecting the whole world. All the institutions, including the church, were turned upside down.

We had to try to figure this out. How could we minister to people? How could we protect people while continuing to help and encourage them? How could we keep the church afloat when no one could attend? Gathering was risky. We were being told not to leave our homes. How could we keep God's people together? How should I lead in a situation I had never faced before?

I had to keep bouncing back.

Emotionally, I felt like a tennis ball, bouncing back and forth from apprehension to reason to responsibility. I had lost my siblings. I had lost my dad. I had lost my wife. My daughter had been through a major surgery to remove a cancerous growth. All of a sudden, with no rest, I was up against the biggest challenge I had ever faced in my thirty years as a pastor. People were looking to me for direction, and all I could do was pray up and man up. It was like the longest, most grueling tennis match you have ever played, with no time to rest.

ANTHONY

Like Venus and Serena Williams at their best. Two powerful forces smashing a tennis ball back and forth. But you're not Venus or Serena. You're the ball.

TONY

An irresistible force meets immovable logic. You're clashing and you still must keep going against these competing forces.

The pandemic disrupted our lives, our work, our play—just like it did yours. There is no more normal. It was a wake-up call and a reminder that God is ultimately in control. It's hard for everyone, but the further you are removed from the Lord, the more chaotic things will become. God is not interested in a pledge of allegiance to a nation; He is interested in a pledge of allegiance to Him. God uses negative events for His purposes. Even if you cannot understand. Even if it seems unfair. Even if you pray without ceasing and it seems as if heaven remains silent.

Sometimes we have to trust God in the dark.

CHRYSTAL

When life comes to a halt, people need hope. They need Jesus, the hope of glory. He is the hope for us all. Jesus Christ calls His church to tell a lost and dying world about the hope we have in Him, which is why our family's life and work centers around bringing His hope through the church.

Church is what we do. We flip on the lights. We sing. We serve. We show up. And when necessary, we pivot. We figure out how to move forward and support others in the church who do the same. We partner with God as He begins a new thing.

How timely was it that we moved from our own unparalleled season of difficulty and pain right into the darkness of a global pandemic? Here's what we have learned and are still learning: God leads you through so you can lead others through. Sometimes you reach back to give someone a hand in a season you've experienced. Other times you offer a hand to someone who's walking through the same season, and you both walk through it together. In either case, you might wonder how you can lead when you yourself are hurting.

> God leads you through so you can lead others through.

You lead by serving others the best you can, as well as you can, and as the Lord leads and your soul lets you—as much as you can. But if I had a nickel for every time someone asked, "Yeah, Chrystal, but how are you doing?"

Dad says it's like playing tennis. I might also say it was like a constant tug-of-war. So, yes, the world stopped in 2020. We all did. But when the world stops, the church keeps going.

JONATHAN

Isaiah 43:19 says God is always doing something new. He makes streams in a dry desert and a path through the wilderness. The verse also asks a very important question.

Are we able to recognize when God is doing a new thing?

CHRYSTAL

The COVID-19 quarantine magnified both the good and the bad. I didn't realize what a support and foundation Mom had been, not only for Daddy's life, but in the life of the church and our ministries as well. That was her space—holding things together. She made it look so easy that it caught us all off guard. We weren't just missing our mother; we were also gaining a new awareness of how big of a role she had played in keeping our ministries going too.

But Mommy is not here now. And as this book is being written, we are still forced to be separate from the normal rhythms of life, from friends, and even from other family members. My parents built our family and church community on the foundation of togetherness. Family and community are what get us through the hard times. But that has changed in 2020.

TONY

The pandemic brought a whole new set of problems that we had to find a way to navigate. We were grieving loss *and* managing a new reality at the same time.

CHRYSTAL

Another thing this season magnified is just how much we are connected with people who care, not just locally, but all over the world. Our family is close, but it's bigger than that. It's the body of Christ. The church stepped up to care for one another and for us.

TONY

On the heels of a viral pandemic we had the loss of George Floyd, which ignited a racial pandemic. That ignited a civil pandemic that involved police and community. Which stirred up what was already an extremely divisive political atmosphere. Medical, racial, civil, social, financial, political—suddenly, we had multiple pandemics all on top of one another.

> **When God allows a divine disruption, it is time for a divine reset.**

Because I believe in the sovereignty of God, my faith affirmed that He had allowed this situation to get our spiritual attention. When God allows a divine disruption, it is time for a divine reset.

ANTHONY

That's a hard one for me, like trying to look at two pictures at the same time. How can one focus on God's sovereignty when there's so much suffering going on?

TONY

Like most churches, we figured out a way to conduct our services online, so I had to preach every week. There I was on the platform preaching on suffering and sovereignty to an empty house. No choir to sing, no ushers down the aisles. Thousands of seats, and no one in them. Everybody stuck at home. You see some strange things in thirty years of ministry, but that might be the strangest. I was like, *Lord, what in the world is going on?*

But as a pastor, I have to preach the good news in whatever situation the people are experiencing. If you are truly called, there is no quit. Regardless of the season, I must bring the Word.

ANTHONY

Tell them about the Temptations, Dad.

TONY

Growing up in Baltimore, my favorite group was the Temptations. Lois and I married in the summer of 1970, and the Temptations had a hit called "Ball of Confusion" that talked about crisis and chaos, cities on fire, destruction everywhere, and panic in the streets. For decades, I have sung that song, not really giving the lyrics much thought. Suddenly, it felt prophetic to me . . .

. . . *and the band played on.*

NINE

MY MOM TOLD ME TO TELL YOU

For I am persuaded that neither death nor life, nor
angels nor rulers, nor things present nor things to
come, nor powers, nor height nor depth, nor any
other created thing will be able to separate us from
the love of God that is in Christ Jesus our Lord.
—ROMANS 8:38–39

JONATHAN

The annual National Religious Broadcasters conference came around again in the spring of 2020, right before the virus shut everything down. NRB held a bittersweet place in my life. It was a reminder that thirty minutes after my father had been inducted into their hall of fame, he was telling us that Mommy's cancer had returned and it was terminal. From the highest mountaintop to the lowest valley in the blink of an eye. I'll probably always associate NRB with that terrible moment. And after our long, traumatic year, it was time for the conference again.

Because our mother had served on the board of directors for many years, the NRB wanted to honor her with a special Heroine of Faith award. Before I found out about the award, my gut instinct was to stay home. We had all been through so much, and I simply wanted as much time as I could possibly get to grieve and recover before I had to be "on" again.

But once they told me how the organization planned to recognize Mom's faithfulness in ministry, I knew I had to press my suit jacket, polish my shoes, and get on a plane to Nashville, the site of the convention.

Janet Parshall, the chairperson of NRB, dedicated Mom's award with these words: "We will forever be impacted by the grace-filled wisdom, compassionate kindness, and gentle Christian witness this precious woman of God brought in her service to the board. Lois was a giant. She filled a room. And when a giant steps out of a room, you note the absence. Lois Evans taught us what it was like to live gracefully."

I had been asked to preach. It had been a long and difficult year since we all watched Dad's induction into the hall of fame, and I had a lot of emotions swirling around inside me as I stood on stage. Before the ceremony, I had watched a 1986 video of my father preaching at NRB. He was thirty-seven years old at the time. I was there, too, just a kid, watching Mom and my big sisters in the hustle and bustle of it all as they handed out cards and sermon tapes.

Now, I was standing before the NRB, and I was thirty-eight years old, a year older than my father had been back then. Talk about nervous! In some ways, I still felt like that kid caught up in all the commotion. I guess you always will when you are walking in your father's footsteps.

I talked to the audience about all the tragedy our family had been through, about my father's induction the year before, how we had gathered in our parents' hotel room after the event for the terrible news. I told them how much that moment hurt, how we all broke down and cried.

Then I told them how my mother had called us in close to deliver a message. She told us that her illness should not stop the ministry from going forward, that the Enemy would take too much pleasure in our discouragement and defeat. She talked about trusting God and moving ahead. Mom assured us that this attack was spiritual warfare and that the Evans family would not turn tail and run.

"Hold up your heads and be strong," she told us. "Continue the work of God."

Mom's words carried a different weight a year later. I am able to process them better now. I believe her words were prophetic, not just for our family and the NRB, but for your family too. I think my mother would want me to deliver the same message to you because everyone reading these words is facing a mountain.

Small or large, a mountain is still a mountain, and you need to hear a word to remind you that no matter what you are going through, no matter what challenges you face in your family, your ministry, your career, or your personal life, you are here to serve the purposes of God. In Deuteronomy 5:32, God told Joshua not to turn aside to the left or the right, because the promised land was right before him

My mother was letting us know that God is allowing things to be shaken because that keeps us moving and clinging to God. Do not quit. Cross your river Jordan. The promised land is too close to turn away now.

In 2 Corinthians 5:10, the apostle Paul said, "We must all appear before the judgment seat of Christ." Sometimes we can get to a place where we are serving religion and ministry instead of serving God. We become so concerned about radio and television broadcasts and social media likes and views that we inadvertently make those things their own gods instead of simply using them as vehicles to serve the one true God.

Whether it's for millions or for a few, the focus is on Christ, who is not concerned about our Sunday-morning numbers or how many followers we have on social media. On that day of accountability, Jesus will ask each of us, "Did you serve the purposes of God?"

Growing up, we had a toy poodle that we named Solomon. I would have chosen something a little tougher, but when you have two older sisters, what can you do? The Bible says King Solomon was one of the wisest men who ever lived. The dog Solomon? Not so wise. I would catch him running in circles, trying to catch his tail. That dog was spending a lot of energy, but he sure wasn't making much progress.

Too often, even under the form of ministry, we are chasing our tails. Expending a lot of energy but not going anywhere, not impressing anyone, not changing anything. Putting on a show for those who are already in the fold.

My father has said, "All these churches, with all these preachers, with all these youth programs, with all these radio and TV programs and conferences and events—and we still have all this mess? There's got to be a dead monkey on the line somewhere. If the church was doing what the church should do, we might not be in this situation."

I know there is great opposition, but we must stay focused and press on if we are to truly impact our generation. Go back to your first love. It's the gospel of Jesus Christ. Philippians 3:13–14 tells us, "I do not consider myself to have taken hold of it. But one thing I do: Forgetting what is behind and reaching forward to what is ahead, I pursue as my goal the prize promised by God's heavenly call in Christ Jesus."

The stories we've shared with you from the last two years show the opposition our family has faced. My dad's younger brother passed away. Six months later he lost his niece. Dad then lost his baby sister, and then her husband died. All of these precious people, saints of God, loved ones dear to our hearts. Two Daddy, my grandfather, passed in November. And a month later, Dad lost his wife and we lost our mom.

Life is painful sometimes. It's hard. Whether it's wayward children or family dysfunction, whether it's finances or sickness or death.

Galatians 6:9 reminds us, "Let us not get tired of doing good, for we will reap at the proper time if we don't give up."

Through thick and thin, drought and flood, good times and bad, even though there's opposition, even though things may not be working out the way we had hoped or planned, we have one goal in this one short life we live on planet earth: *Do not lose focus. Serve the purposes of God.*

My mother told me to tell you that.

We have one goal in this one short life we live on planet earth: *Do not lose focus. Serve the purposes of God.*

PART TWO

RESOLVE, REBUILD, RETROFIT

We are afflicted in every way but not crushed; we are perplexed but not in despair; we are persecuted but not abandoned; we are struck down but not destroyed. We always carry the death of Jesus in our body, so that the life of Jesus may also be displayed in our body. For we who live are always being given over to death for Jesus' sake, so that Jesus' life may also be displayed in our mortal flesh. So then, death is at work in us, but life in you. And since we have the same spirit of faith in keeping with what is written, I believed, therefore I spoke, we also believe, and therefore speak. For we know that the one who raised the Lord Jesus will also raise us with Jesus and present us with you. Indeed, everything is for your benefit so that, as grace extends through more and more people, it may cause thanksgiving to increase to the glory of God.

Therefore we do not give up. Even though our outer person is being destroyed, our inner person is being renewed day by day. For our momentary light affliction is producing

for us an absolutely incomparable eternal weight of glory. So
we do not focus on what is seen, but on what is unseen. For
what is seen is temporary, but what is unseen is eternal.
—2 CORINTHIANS 4:8-18

Love God, love each other, and help people. Do
this and your living will never be in vain.
—DR. TONY EVANS

The man who kneels to God can stand up to anything.
—DR. LOIS EVANS

---------------------------------- TEN ----------------------------------

IS HE GOD OR NOT?

But if it doesn't please you to worship the Lᴏʀᴅ, choose
for yourselves today: Which will you worship—the gods
your ancestors worshiped beyond the Euphrates River
or the gods of the Amorites in whose land you are living?
As for me and my family, we will worship the Lᴏʀᴅ.

—JOSHUA 24:15

ANTHONY

My siblings and I grew up in the suburbs of Dallas, Texas. One of the highlights of our summers was spending the day at Six Flags Over Texas, an amusement park that was a quick thirty-minute drive from home. Looking back as an adult, I cannot imagine how we got any pleasure out of standing in line for two hours for a minute-and-a-half ride on Yosemite Sam and the Gold River Adventure. Have you ever been to Texas in the summer? It's like 105 degrees with 1,000 percent humidity, and Six Flags is two hundred acres of concrete and steel.

But, whatever. We were kids, and we *loved* going to Six Flags, laughing and acting crazy with our friends, eating Dippin' Dots, and riding all the rides. Our favorite was the Shock Wave, a double-loop roller coaster that was once upon a time one of the tallest and fastest in the world.

One day we hit the front gate as soon as the park opened, and we made a mad dash for the Shock Wave before there was a line. Sure enough, not one person was there before us. Front car! It wasn't even that hot out yet.

We whizzed through the turnstiles toward the launch station. Finally, the bright-blue coaster was in sight. That's when I noticed a yellow rope blocking the entrance. A sign hanging from the rope informed us that the ride was closed.

About then, someone wearing Six Flags coveralls with the word "Engineer" on the back walked by with a toolbox in his hand. Because I am inquisitive by nature and I don't just accept things without knowing why, I asked, "Hey, why is the Shock Wave shut down? This is what we came here for."

"Yeah, there's some stuff we gotta adjust and check out," he said. "Sorry, but we can't do any type of maintenance when the ride is running."

Anxious, inquiring minds want to know more, so I asked, "When will it be done? Ten minutes? An hour? By the end of the day for sure, right?" I must drive people crazy with all my questions.

"Well, we have to take our time," the engineer explained. "It won't be today. Or even tomorrow. Actually, this roller coaster will probably be closed for several days. See, we're turning you and your buddies upside down twice in an open-air car that's going sixty miles per hour. So we have to make absolutely sure that every tiny bolt, screw, and wheel on this thing is safe and secure."

I stood there and thought about what the engineer had said. On the one hand, I was disappointed. We had gotten up early, booked it across town, and run through the park with high hopes of being first on the Shock Wave. On the other hand, I knew what he was telling me was not only true, but it was for my own good. I was simply going to have to wait. Once I calmed down, I realized I did not want to ride some crazy double-loop roller coaster if it needed maintenance.

One time a friend of mine got stuck going up the Shock Wave's first hill. You know the really big one that seems like forever to get up before you take what normally is the biggest dive down into the rest of the ride. Some Six Flags staffers had to climb up and undo the harnesses so everybody could climb back down. Know why? Something needed maintenance.

So I had to decide something that morning. Did I believe the engineer knew what he was talking about or not?

In the same way, we have to make a decision concerning God, the One who engineered our minds, bodies, and spirits, the Creator who makes the wheels of the universe turn. Can we take Him at His word? Does He know what He is talking about or not? Because life can be a lot like that roller coaster. It moves fast and whips you every which way, and none of us want to fall out when everything turns upside down.

When you feel like your life has shut down and you have to wait, do you trust the Engineer? When the ride has been disrupted, are you going to have faith that God is still in control?

JONATHAN

Is He God or not? This is the question we must ask and answer for ourselves.

I have found that God is *never* not God, even when you feel like He's not operating in the way you had hoped. For instance, take our family losses, in particular the loss of our mom. We all felt the depth of pain when we realized our prayers were not being answered in the way we hoped they would be. But it was not up to us. God is not someone we can manipulate or change. He has His own plan. We can humbly approach with our own hopes and dreams, but He will always come through in His own way and in His own time for the purposes of His kingdom. So even though I am part of His kingdom, I do not get to define what that kingdom is or how it works.

This is all about trust. Learning to trust is a process. It takes time. And thank God, His mercy is new each morning. Emotions come and go based on circumstances. God sees the big picture, past the emotions, beyond circumstances. The God we serve is faithful in good times and in bad. He is not interested in those who only offer thanks when everything goes their way. God desires that we come to Him whether we face catastrophe or enjoy prosperity, pain or joy, sickness or health. We boldly approach the throne because He is our Father and He wants us all to Himself.

> **So is He God or not? We answer this question daily, with every minute and hour that passes.**

So is He God or not? We answer this question daily, with every minute and hour that passes. Whether times are good or bad, we are to respond to His call.

PRISCILLA

If God is so good and powerful, why do bad things happen?

As a person in ministry, I get asked some version of this question frequently. To be honest, I've pondered it as well. During this time of widespread crises, which has been characterized by so much loss, grief, and confusion on a global scale, it is an understandable concern. And yet I wonder if the question itself lacks balance and insight.

I find that we are often quick to blame God for anything bad that happens, calling His character and kindness into question at the first sign of trouble. But we aren't always so swift to credit Him with *everything* good, even the ordinary goodness that underscores our daily lives. While I would never want to minimize the pain and disappointment that life's messy moments cause us, the reality is that it is *because of* His abundant goodness, love for us, and mighty power that we experience any type of peace, hope, and calm in our lives at all. We are sin sick, and the world in which we live is saturated with evil. It is only by the power of His restraint that this evil doesn't break through into our experience every second of each day.

Because He is good.

Think about it like this: if you've ever been to the ocean, then you know the overwhelming and awe-inspiring feeling of seeing the vastness of its mighty waves. You know what it's like to realize that the sea is far deeper, more powerful, and more mysterious than any human will likely ever be able to comprehend. Without the restraint of the land on which we stand, the miles-deep water would surely overtake the entirety of society, consuming and swallowing everything in its path.

But Job 38:10–11 reminds us that our mighty Father "locked it behind barred gates, limiting its shores." He said, "This far and no farther will you come. Here your proud waves must stop!" (NLT). If God were to remove His hand, endless tsunamis would devastate our land. The only reason the ocean does not completely overtake the earth is because God's power holds it back.

Day after ordinary day when you did not receive the grim diagnosis, when your loved one did not succumb to death, when betrayal did not poison your relationship, when the accident did not total your possessions, this was by His power alone, holding back the endless waves of evil pressing in on your life.

And when, in His sovereignty, He allows difficulty to seep in, that is not a sign of powerlessness or forgetfulness or lovelessness. It is because, for reasons we may never fully understand on this side of eternity, His glory will be best magnified, His good purposes fully come to pass, and His character in us more completely developed because of that hardship. Either way, He is still God, and we can still trust Him with our whole hearts and lives.

If ever that theory became reality to me, it was during this extended season of difficulty for my family, coupled with the disturbing era of global dysfunction in which we all live now. Have we felt uneasy? Oh, yes. Devastated even. Have we cried? Many, many tears. Did we have to regroup, refocus, and start again? Yes, and in so many ways we still are.

I'm sure there will likely be more tears to wipe away, more anxieties to quell, and more chances to start all over once again. We will wrestle and struggle and ask God questions. Thankfully, God knows our frame and doesn't mind our questions. He is well acquainted with our weaknesses, having taken on human form. Jesus knows hurt, He knows our tears, He knows disappointment. And our beautiful Savior empathizes with us.

> **Jesus knows hurt, He knows our tears, He knows disappointment. And our beautiful Savior empathizes with us.**

More than ever before, I am grateful for my godly parents who modeled what it looks like to trust God even when times are hard. While they may have asked God questions, they never questioned His character, even when they did not understand His choices. They kept on praying, resting, and claiming confidence in Him. They believed that, though circumstances may have changed, our God does not.

I believe that too.

Our hope is not rooted in delusion; rather it is a holy optimism stirred by the Holy Spirit within. Suffering and adversity have not changed the nature of God, nor have they canceled out the hope we have in Jesus. Instead, they have cemented my confidence in Him. I still endure pain and breathlessness from the surgery that removed a part of my lung. But each time I feel my respiratory system working hard to sustain me, I am grateful for each breath He gives me, and I remember that this planet is not my home. I have a new body waiting on me in heaven. The same kind my momma got the moment she stepped into glory. The same kind my beloved mother-in-law, Mary, received when she met Mom there eight months later.

The only way a human being can stay steady and hope-filled through life and death is by firmly believing that God is still in charge, that He loves us unflinchingly, and that Jesus has gone ahead to prepare a place for us. That's how my mother and mother-in-law lived their lives, and it's how they finished strong. They were talking about Jesus until they no longer had the strength to speak. Their eyes were firmly fixed on that place that Jesus had prepared for them.

One day, close to the end of my mother's life, she was in a wheelchair because of malnutrition, barely able to walk or even talk. And through her weak, broken, gibberish words, she tried to ask Dad, "At what point will I be in heaven? When will I actually see Jesus? Will my soul leave my body so that I can see Him? Will there be any delay?"

Dad did not have detailed answers for that. He could only tell Mom what he knew from Scripture, but he encouraged her. And in doing so, he encouraged us all. He reminded us that 2 Corinthians 5:8 says that to be absent from the body is to be present with the Lord. We were facing immense tragedy, but in that difficult time, our confidence in this reality gave us hope and refreshed our tired, worn souls. My mother never doubted she was on her way to heaven. She was only curious as to how it would all unfold. I watched my mother face death with hope. And I saw that hope carry her across. I want that same hope to carry me too.

My mother taught me many things in life. But the most powerful lesson she showed me was how to die well, with my eyes fixed on Jesus.

CHRYSTAL

Mom and I were watching Priscilla walk the red carpet at the premiere of one of her movies. I looked at Mommy and said, "Priscilla's been on the red carpet her whole life." I was just joking, but it was true. Priscilla is the super-confident, always-together sister. Gymnastics, beauty pageants, cheerleading, spelling bees—Silla was constantly winning at whatever she set out to do. And if anything *is* wrong, you will never know it from her. I think she was born that way.

Me? I'm not quite that together all the time. I'm just saying, You might see some coffee stains on my jeans. But the work will be done, the kids will be fed, and there will be a few thousand people watching me on my Livestream as I sit at my desk and share wisdom from home.

Sometimes life is crazy. I've usually got so many things going on at once that you might find me running behind and scrambling to catch up. Just ask Anthony. He moves really fast, and we have to constantly talk about his pace versus mine.

And if something is wrong or it doesn't make sense to me, I have to talk about it. You'll definitely know if something is out of sorts with me. I have to take my time and walk through things as I try to make sense of them in my heart and mind.

I don't think there is anything wrong with me or the way I'm wired. I believe that the God who wants us to have confidence in Him is also Jesus, the same God in human flesh whose close friend pleaded in Mark 9:24, "Help my unbelief." I believe confidence and a desire for more clarity can coexist.

> The God who wants us to have confidence in Him is also Jesus, the same God in human flesh whose close friend pleaded in Mark 9:24, "Help my unbelief."

I'd be lying if I said I never struggle with God's decision not to heal my mother on this side of heaven. I do. Often. I'm not in a place of unwavering faith all day, every day. But I believe God knows me deeply and is willing to walk with me, even when I'm feeling my way through.

But I also come from a ministry family. People look to us for hope. So what happens when you beg God with every ounce of faith you've got, and your prayer still doesn't get answered? How do you get your hopes back up and go forth with confidence after your heart has been crushed? If someone comes to me hurt, confused, and struggling to believe, what can I possibly offer that is personal and real from my own point of view?

I can offer honesty. My honest struggle with God, often in real time, and my commitment to a God whose heart I trust even when I can't see His hand.

For me, it's not a matter of whether I believe He is God or not; it's a choice. I choose to believe He is.

The struggle is real. This life is a fight. But I believe truth can still reside in the struggle we all share. And I also believe that God meets us when we are honest and real.

What kinds of honest questions do you have? Do you believe that God has His own reasons to allow what He allows, regardless of whether we understand?

For instance, do you believe that the loved ones we lose close their eyes and cease to exist? That my mother who has passed from this life and I will never cross paths again? Or would we rather believe she will live through me and in me as I finish my days on earth and that her fingerprints are everywhere, even in her absence, giving life to those who remain? That we will meet again in a place where there is no more sadness or loss or pain? That Mommy is home with Jesus, and everything we loved about her is alive and well even now?

I choose to believe. And I choose to believe in God who gives me this hope. I choose honesty, too, and acknowledge that my belief in God is not without questions.

Our hearts are made to long for hope. First Peter 1:3 says that we can be filled with "living hope through the resurrection of Jesus Christ from the dead." That is what I cling to, even though the storm hits like a hurricane, even when the wind and rain beat me down. I hold on to that rock.

Verse 22 of Jude tells us to be merciful to those who question and doubt. I need that mercy. You might too. People are messy. We tend to find what we focus on.

Proverbs 11:27 says that those who look for good find favor, while trouble comes for those who always see the negative side. First Thessalonians 5:16–18 reminds us that part of our mission down here is to pursue love, pray nonstop, rejoice always, and give thanks in all things. This means I have to work hard not to focus on my questions and doubts.

In all the suffering and stress of the last few years, I have tried to be intentional about highlighting the tiny specks of diamond in the dirt. I think about moments like Mom's night out at Kingdom Legacy Live. God gave us that night together, and it was so good. If that event had happened a few days before or after, she wouldn't have been able to come.

Even the timing of her passing, difficult as it was, had a sweetness to it. We had one last Christmas together. The church was packed for her homecoming celebration because it was still during the holidays and everyone had not yet returned to work. As much as I would have loved for her to be with us longer, had God answered that prayer, we wouldn't have been able to honor her life the way we did if that had happened during the quarantine.

Mommy left on a high note. She finished well. I can't imagine her having to fight cancer during the pandemic. She would have been so sick and so worried about Dad. I can't imagine laying our mother to rest during the lockdown. I know many have experienced that, and I know it deepens the pain in an already difficult season. I also know my mother would not have wanted us to have to fuss with all of that.

Mom made it to Christmas, and then she went home. That is not the way we wanted the story to end. But as endings go, it worked out okay. God, in all His grace, gave us good moments. God didn't answer our prayers for healing, but He was still good in the provisions of His choosing. I am thankful for those small moments of grace. There is a time to wrestle with God and a time when He leads us to rest.

> **The God who allows sorrows is the God of sweet new seasons too.**

The passage of time gives us perspective. We discover that life moves on and that our hearts can heal. The sun rises, and the world keeps turning. Babies are born and flowers bloom and there is always something starting new again. The God who allows sorrows is the God of sweet new seasons too.

I am determined to look for the good. I cannot stop or give up now. Mark 9:24 says, "I do believe; help my unbelief!" And 1 Thessalonians 5:18 encourages us to give thanks to God in all things.

More than ever, I realize He is truly all I have.

Confidence in Christ is what I choose. Born that way? Maybe not. Reborn to believe? Absolutely!

TONY

I have always believed that God is sovereign, even in the midst of bad times. Nothing happens that does not first pass through the hands of God. Within that sovereignty, I have to function in a way that seeks to glorify Him and bring good to others.

Anyone who has answered God's call knows that ministry does not stop when life gets hard. People still need hope and help, and honestly, that calling kept me moving forward. In fact, it helped me stay afloat. I firmly believe that serving others is a key to enduring in difficult times. When we minister to the hurting and lost, God ministers to us. By blessing, we are blessed. I pressed on toward the mark promised by God's call because it brought me great joy and purpose to continue to help others. The race was not over. I had to get up and keep running.

I know there is a legitimate concern for ministry burnout. I realize preachers need to rest too. But I'm just telling you, it helped me to show up every week on Sunday, to be there for God's people, to prepare and preach the Word. Teaching and preaching reminded me of what I hope for and where my hope lies. First John 2:17 tells us this world and its desires pass away, "but the one who does the will of God remains forever."

I firmly believe that serving others is a key to enduring in difficult times.

It's easy to praise the Lord when all is well and life is good, prayers are answered, miracles are witnessed, victories are won. We get confused about God when the opposite occurs. But God is God in good times and bad. In Job 13:15, Job said, "Though He slay me, yet will I trust Him" (NKJV). True faith praises through the storm. Job went to a whole lot of funerals in a short amount of time too.

Also, I realize that the way I live my life affects others. James 3:1 says that preachers are held to a higher standard. I've got a lot of eyes on me during a crisis, watching to see how I hold up. If I stumble, I may cause others to do so as well. Not that I grit my teeth and become a martyr. I press on, not only for family and my church, but also for myself.

God's grace and blessing ever flow. I serve others, doing my best to live in a manner worthy of the calling. God blesses me. Out of that blessing, I continue to serve others even more. And God continues to bless. Living water is never stagnant. It flows persistently, streams into rivers into the sea.

In this life there will be sorrow and pain. Wars will be fought. Disease will spread. Conflicts rise. But I would rather face crisis with God than have to face it alone.

---------- E L E V E N ----------

GETTING OUR ATTENTION

But in their distress they turned to the Lord, the God of
Israel, and sought him, and he was found by them.
—2 CHRONICLES 15:4 NIV

TONY

I believe the global predicament with COVID-19 is far more than just a medical crisis. In fact, everything we are facing—economic crises, political crises, financial crises, familial crises—goes much deeper than what's on the surface. Everything visible and physical is preceded by that which is invisible and spiritual. If you want to address the visible and physical, you must identify the cause and cure to that which is invisible and spiritual. To put it another way, if all you see is what you see, then you do not see all that there is to be seen.

I believe this disruption we are experiencing has been allowed in order to precipitate a spiritual realignment and center us back toward God. Second Chronicles 15:5–6 says, "In those times there was no peace for those who went about their daily activities because the residents of the lands had many conflicts. Nation was crushed by nation and city by city, for God troubled them with every possible distress."

In these verses the Bible describes a world in chaos and individuals without peace. When the people of Judah and Benjamin went home, there was family conflict. City rose up against city and nation against nation. There was no peace in the land.

At the end of verse 6 it says, "For God troubled them with every possible distress." Wait a minute. Who is behind this chaos and lack of peace? The Lord took the blame.

In the Old Testament, when God's people departed from Him, judgment followed soon behind. With the sacrifice of Jesus, God recast His relationship to the world. Second Corinthians 5:19 says that the world was reconciled to God through the death of Jesus Christ.

No longer does the Lord God rain down fire and brimstone or send floods, like in Noah's day, but we can experience the passive wrath of God that is described in Romans 1:24, 26, 28. The Scripture says that God turned them over to impurity. Then, again, later in the chapter, God turned them over to disgraceful passions. A third time, God turned them over to a corrupt mind.

Because the people of God no longer took Him seriously, choosing to dishonor Him and drift away, He let them experience the consequences of their behavior and see what life looked like without His provision.

Romans 1:21–24 describes what happens when an individual, family, church, or nation depart from God: "For although they knew God, they neither glorified him as God nor gave thanks to him, but their thinking became futile and their foolish hearts were darkened. Although they claimed to be wise, they became fools and exchanged the glory of the immortal God for images made to look like a mortal human being and birds and animals, and reptiles. Therefore, God gave them over in the sinful desires of their hearts" (NIV).

The great seventeenth-century French mathematician, physicist, philosopher, and theologian Blaise Pascal recognized the void everyone feels in a crisis. His insight has been summarized in the popular saying that "there is a God-shaped vacuum in the human heart that cannot be satisfied by any created thing but only by God the Creator, who is made known through Jesus Christ."

When we stray from God, the vacuum returns, whether in the heart of a nation or the heart of man. Nature abhors a vacuum, and that empty space will soon be filled. I would like to suggest that the crisis we are experiencing is due to the absence of God. Global catastrophes, unrest, anxiety, fear, sickness—these things are rushing to fill the vacuum we have caused by departing from God.

Yes, we know God exists everywhere, but I am talking about the relational absenteeism of God. It is as if God has said, *If you don't want Me, you're going to have to see what life is like without Me.* So I believe God is interrupting the normal, natural, and preferred order of things on every single level. God is sending a worldwide message.

Returning to the Old Testament story, 2 Chronicles 15:3 speaks to the causes of the chaos and crisis at that time: "For many years Israel has been without the true God, without a teaching priest, and without instruction."

He didn't say there was no *belief* in God; he said their belief was not in "the true God." The Israelites had replaced "the true God" with idols.

An idol is not simply a golden statue. It is any person, place, thing, or thought that takes the place of God. The greatest sin in all of the Bible is idolatry because you have removed God's exclusivity clause: no competitors allowed!

Idols can be sophisticated, not just a golden calf or a pillar erected in homage to a foreign god. Technology, money, people, relationships, they can all take the place of God. Politics or sex can become an idol. Career or education can turn into idolatry. Even family or religion can be an idol.

Whatever is placed alongside of or in front of God as He has revealed Himself will be rejected by Him. This opens a hole for corrupt things to enter that space.

We are living in a day when God has been put on a loop, like the highways that circle a city. These freeways are close enough to the center of a city to get you there quickly but far enough away to keep you from getting bogged down in downtown traffic. Spiritually speaking, we want God, but we want Him to be on the loop around our lives. Close enough to make us seem respectable, but far enough away that He doesn't get entangled with the details of our lives. We want to be able to reference Him on Sunday, but we don't need His information, direction, or decrees on Monday. We want a God we can fist bump, one who shows up in a quick prayer or social media post but who stays out of our business and our lives. So even when we are singing songs and going to church, we do not wind up with the true God.

> **We want a God we can fist bump, one who shows up in a quick prayer or social media post but who stays out of our business and our lives.**

Why does 2 Chronicles say there was no true God? Verse 3 says this happened because there was no teaching priest. Please note the verse doesn't say that there weren't *any* priests. It says that the priests weren't teaching anything worthwhile. They were not pointing people to the one true God. You can be assured that a mist in the pulpit will always create a fog in the pew. When pastors and leaders fail to point people to the uncompromising truth of God, the natural outcome will be that the culture will become confused, and the society will begin to decline.

Many of our churches have failed as they have bowed to culture and dumbed down His deity by ignoring His Word. We are no longer teaching unapologetic truth. We are teaching what we think or what feels good to the people. We teach what is popular and preferred.

There are two answers to every question: God's answer and everybody else's. And everybody else is wrong. God has spoken and He does not stutter. His Word is perfection, ever relevant, speaking to all issues, for all of life.

God defines marriage. God defines gender. God defines identity. God defines what it means to be parents and how children should respond. God defines religion and how the church operates. He creates and defines governments and how they should be run. He has spoken on how the citizens of a nation are supposed to act. God defines sexuality. We don't. When we start to redefine seminal issues like these, chaos will ensue.

In creating our own rules and parameters, we insult God. When there are no teaching priests in the land and the pulpits allow society to vote on what God has said, we do not conform to God's standard. We only make people comfortable with their own standards.

God speaks to the issues of righteousness and justice and how to handle the poor, pursue equity, and stabilize economic structures and personal finances. The mission of a teaching priest is to declare God's truth with love and clarity on every issue in society.

God's Word must become the current standard by which all issues are addressed, by which all people must conform, and by which all systems must be adjusted. No matter how high or how low, regardless of political, social, or economic position, the teaching priest must never kowtow to the culture. The leader must speak with spiritual authority and Holy Ghost power.

The best way for the servants of God to love and care for the people is to speak God's truth. The pulpit must preach in a way that overrides the opinions of society or what your parents may have taught you. God's Word must override what professors or politicians have to say. It overrules what the media is trying to promote. We have no more time for clever sermonettes or cute Christian phrases. This is a season for preaching the full counsel of God's Word with grace but without apology.

Finally, the passage from 2 Chronicles says there was no instruction.

In other words, the people had no guidelines to govern their actions. It is equivalent to the modern encouragement to honor your *own* truth. This is what I think, this is how I feel, this is what I believe. So this is my truth.

But our truth cannot disagree with God's truth. When we do this, we call God a liar. We elevate our thoughts, opinions, and wisdom higher than His. When opinions are god, confusion reigns and people are troubled by every kind of distress.

Thankfully, 2 Chronicles 15:4 gives us a solution: "But when they turned to the Lord God of Israel in their distress and sought Him, He was found by them."

Do you see that? "In their *distress*." And we know from verse 6 that "God troubled them with every possible distress." God will allow the levels of chaos to rise until He gets our undivided attention, not because He is cruel, but because He desires our wholehearted allegiance. We do that with our own children sometimes, right? We make things inconvenient until they pay attention.

"They turned to the Lord God of Israel in their distress and sought Him."

You know what God wants? A return to Him in our personal lives, our families, our churches, and our government. Yes, even the government. Let us not forget what the Lord says in Romans 13:1: "There is no authority except from God, and the authorities that exist are instituted by God."

It's an agenda from hell when we allow the government to divide the church. God created governments. He doesn't just want a name check and quick introductory prayer. God wants to set society's agenda. He wants conformity to His will, submission to His authority, and a relationship with us as His people.

The question is, How do you seek Him? Here's how: you pursue a relationship while submitting to His authority, and just like with the children of Israel, He will let you find Him.

The desire of God is relationship with His people. Make knowing Him your goal. This is done only by the Lord Jesus Christ. The Son of the living God. He lived a perfect life, and then He died a substitutionary death in your place for your sins to give you the gift of eternal life and connect you with the Father.

Anyone who comes to Christ for the forgiveness of sins and the gift of eternal life will freely receive. You cannot earn it. He's giving it away. As you cultivate that relationship, God will speak peace while we wait on Him to solve our problems.

> The desire of God is relationship with His people. Make knowing Him your goal.

Psalm 46:1 tells us He is our refuge and strength, an ever-present help in times of distress. The Lord knows that as long as there is no discomfort, you will stay on your side. You will not cling to Him.

I believe God has allowed distress in my life and yours because He wants us to move closer to Him. Now is the time to run to Him, seek Him, pursue Him, be passionate after Him, come to know Him through His Son. To get into His Word and grow in your commitment to Him. And then to submit to His Word whether you feel like it or not. Our feelings must be the caboose, not the engine.

God will bless us, our families, and our culture as we learn that the God who causes distress also alleviates the distress when we return to His side.

TWELVE

GOOD NEWS ON GOOD FRIDAY

Because of the LORD's faithful love
we do not perish,
for his mercies never end.
They are new every morning;
great is your faithfulness!
I say, "The LORD is my portion,
therefore I will put my hope in him."
—LAMENTATIONS 3:22–24

CHRYSTAL

Easter 2020 came, and everything in the world was still so strange. We were all processing our grief in our own ways, trying to get a handle on life during a pandemic and ministry under a lockdown. It was also our first Easter without her. The first few months of 2020 had given us a new revelation as to just how much Mommy worked faithfully behind the scenes to support us and keep the family moving on. We missed her—because she was our mother, of course, but also because she was the backbone of so much of the ministry in our family.

It was a weird season of both anxiety and rest. Forced rest, I guess, because of the pandemic. It wasn't long before I started to feel restless. I noticed that other people were feeling restless too. On a whim, I decided to jump online and livestream every morning—a cup of coffee in hand—and talk through it. The chats were unscripted and at times brutally honest. The more honest I was about my mindset and emotions, the more others felt invited to do the same as they commented and connected while watching my videos. I eventually decided to invite people to join me on screen for these honest conversations to discuss their personal trials and triumphs of the season.

One of my favorite morning conversations was with my dad. So many people wanted to know how I was doing—how we were all doing—and I thought it would be good for the two of us to have coffee and talk about the very real and unexpected craziness that we had been facing in public and in private. Life is so busy. Even during the pandemic, there was ministry to do, and I didn't want to get too distracted and let time slip away. I didn't want to wait until it was too late to make important statements or ask important questions. I also didn't want to miss the opportunity to seek Daddy's wisdom and insight and share it with others who might need it too.

People all across the world were talking about family, about getting back to the basics, returning both to God and to a slower way of life. It's a shame it took a worldwide plague to wake some of us up, but no matter how it happens, when hearts turn to Jesus, it's a hopeful thing. And if anyone knows about hope in hard times, it's my dad. So, I asked him to join me, and he agreed to meet me one morning, both of us with coffee in hand.

CHRYSTAL

Hey, Daddy! Thanks for getting up so early.

TONY

[Laughs] Well, thank you for forcing me to get up.

CHRYSTAL

Come on, Daddy, you know you wanted to get up at the crack of dawn and join me for a live video conversation [laughing too]. We're doing this because you and I have been holding on to hope in recent days, and there are a bunch of people who are in need of hope too. Daddy, if there is one thing I know for sure about you, it's that you are a hope giver. You are such a naturally optimistic person, and you create a sense of expectation about God's moving, even when we can't see Him, even if we can't make sense of things. It's Good Friday, so we think of Jesus and His death on the cross. But we call it Good Friday because good news was on the way. We've been through so much these last two years. You lost a niece, two siblings, your brother-in-law, your father, and my mom, your wife. I know you stay busy, but we worry about you sometimes. Can I ask a real question and ask you to give me a real answer? How are you dealing with things? I know you trust God, but are you really okay?

TONY

Each day has its ups and downs, and all I can really do is take them one day at a time. Things are different now, for sure. I have times of loneliness. But there are also many good memories and a lot to be grateful for. I'm surrounded by the love and support from my family as well as my family of faith.

Forty-nine years of marriage. We nearly made it to fifty, and I am eternally grateful for all the blessings in those years. While I miss

Mommy, I am thankful for her investment in me and my ministry. She left her footprints everywhere. I would not be doing ministry at this level without the grace of God and the support of Lois Evans. But, yes, God is leading me into a new season. So I am trusting Him for new mercies every day and every step of the way.

CHRYSTAL

So many people watched us pray for Mommy's healing. But that is not what God chose on this side of heaven. Remember that day a couple of months ago when I was in Mom's closet and you asked how I was doing? I usually just give a quick "fine." I may not be, but because I know you're grieving, too, I don't want to burden you with all my emotions all of the time. As a pastor, you have so much on you, so many people looking to you for support.

But that day, I just couldn't do it. I couldn't hold it in. All the questions came pouring out. We had so many signs that pointed toward healing, so much light along the way that gave us hope. But Mom wasn't getting better. I was so disappointed and confused. And you let me talk that day. You listened. You let me ask all of my questions and then you said, "I have those same questions too." It helped to hear you admit you were struggling. But even in struggle and disappointment, you believed. When God doesn't answer the biggest, most important prayer request of your life, how does that not damage your faith?

TONY

You always have to go back to the character of God. If you lose sight of God's character, you will be lost. Life has things that we can never understand, but His will is inscrutable.

In the Old Testament, the prophet Habakkuk struggled with what

God was allowing to happen. In Habakkuk 1:2, he asked the age-old question *why*, and then the prophet asked, "How long, LORD, must I call for help and you do not listen?"

But in chapter 3, verses 17–18, Habakkuk made a profound statement: "Though the fig tree does not bud and there is no fruit on the vines, though the olive crop fails and the fields produce no food, though the flocks disappear from the pen and there are no herds in the stalls, yet I will celebrate in the LORD; I will rejoice in the God of my salvation!"

> You always have to go back to the character of God. If you lose sight of God's character, you will be lost.

In other words, Habakkuk had to resign himself to who God was when he could not make sense of what God was doing. Isaiah 40 is my go-to passage when people cry out to God and wonder why. And God says that His understanding is unfathomable and that there are things about Him that we will never be able to understand.

So I appeal to what I know to be true about God's character. He is good. He is sovereign. There are things He does not reveal. Job never found out why he suffered so much struggle and loss. What sustained him through suffering and loss was his knowledge of God. And at the end of his conversation with God in Job 42:5, Job said, "I had heard reports about you, but now my eyes have seen you."

My passion is to see God in the things that I am able to understand. That's where my comfort comes from in the midst of loss.

CHRYSTAL

What does it mean to see God apart from what you've known about Him? What does that look like practically for you? I'm not sure I know how to believe God beyond my experience.

TONY

These days there's a lot of time with just me and God, more so than when I am busy. In a strange way, the pandemic has helped because I've had to reset my pace and slow down. Every morning I am walking through passages of Scripture, just reading and thinking. I'm not preparing for a sermon or a Bible class. I'm doing it for me. And I am asking God to give me a greater sense of His presence, of His power, and of His will.

According to Isaiah 40:29–31, one of the ways we get to see God is when He gives us new strength to carry on. The Holy Spirit brings comfort. He gives peace even when you have tears. I hear God speaking to my soul and reminding me that it's okay. I'm finding things Lois said or wrote that I never knew about before. People call to testify about her impact on their lives. They remind me of her faith. Lois said that I had to keep going. There's still work to be done. So, with God's help, I press on toward the goal for which He has called me through Christ Jesus.

> God is close to the brokenhearted. He understands our pain. While I would like more answers, I have decided to trust Him.

God is close to the brokenhearted. He understands our pain. While I would like more answers, I have decided to trust Him.

CHRYSTAL

Mommy passed on December 30, and you preached the message at church on New Year's Eve. Can I tell you that all of your children were like, "Uh, Dad? You think maybe you should be still for a while and give yourself some space to mourn?" But the pandemic has given us all plenty of space, hasn't it?

TONY

In Psalm 23:2, the psalmist said, "He lets me lie down in green pastures; he leads me beside quiet waters." But you know what? It hasn't been too bad. I have been able to kick back a little, rest more than I normally would. One thing I never seemed to have time for was reading. Now I can. It's a time of rest and restoration.

CHRYSTAL

For those of us who always complain about needing more time with our kids, well, our prayers have been answered, haven't they? I'm not saying God caused all this illness and unrest, but only something this drastic would force us to slow down. Sometimes busyness becomes an idol. A lot of us are sick with too much stress, too much work, not enough time with family and God. When you slow down, you focus more on what is important. A lot of people are using this opportunity to seek God and try to figure out how that works.

TONY

It's like exercising. The hardest part is starting. You don't have to run a marathon the first morning. Run five minutes and walk a little. Just get moving. A little bit on a regular schedule is better than a whole lot occasionally.

Prayer is not some formal display. It's a conversation, just like this.

Get your coffee, have a seat, and say, "Okay, God. Let's talk." Tell Him how you feel, what you're thinking, what you are struggling with today. I love that the Lord's Prayer begins with the words "Our Father." Jesus said we can start with "Hello, Dad." We can talk to God as we would a father.

Jesus is the living Word. When the written Word connects with the living Word, then you have the life-giving Word. That time will become precious because you're engaging the Lord through His Word in relationship, communication, and conversation. If we ask God, He will speak.

CHRYSTAL

Daddy, the way you've made yourself available has helped me feel comfortable talking to God in the same way. I can see Him as a loving father because I've had you. And you have always been about my personal and spiritual development. I still have the Bible you gave me in sixth grade, the one with Jesus the Shepherd on the front. Inside, it says "To my beloved daughter." You have always been here and made yourself available to me and allowed me to ask you questions. But what about people who don't have a good relationship with their father?

TONY

I get this question all the time. You don't have to limit your definition of father to your biological dad. Is there anyone in your circle you see as a great example of a father? There are others who can fill that gap.

But don't start with your father and transfer that image to God. Start with God, and transfer that back to you. If you're using your earthly father as a point of reference, then it's easy to dismiss God. Reading John 1:18, we know that Jesus came to reveal the Father. Go through John's Gospel and note how Jesus talked about His relationship with His Father. Ask the Lord to show you His fatherhood and experience His reality as your Dad. Start where you can, and it will grow. God will father you.

CHRYSTAL

People ask how our family stays tight. Four kids, all in ministry, all following the Lord. I always tell them it was you and Mom. You were the same at home as you were at church. Mommy made sure that we always gathered around the dinner table as a family. Sure, you were busy with church, but you were never too busy to play and horse around with us. And you were never too busy to talk or listen or encourage. And I know I talked a lot!

Family first

TONY

The number-one thing a man can do for his children is to take the dinner table seriously. Psalm 128:3 says, "Your children [will be] like young olive trees around your table." In the Bible, the family table was not just for eating but for leading. Turn off the television, get rid of the devices that steal attention. As you eat, you lead, you speak to each child, you look them in the eye, you express value. Prayer is not simply blessing the food. You bless the family.

If you spend an hour a day around the table, you can change the direction of your whole family. And of course, you talk and share your life. You find out who your kids are spending time with, what's going on at school. Men, please do not lay all that responsibility on your wives. Know your children. Get involved in their world. Busy as ministry can be, I almost always drove my kids to school. We would pray together just before I dropped you all off.

> If you spend an hour a day around the table, you can change the direction of your whole family.

CHRYSTAL

You would come to my track meets. Before each race, I would look into the stands and find you. There you were, cheering me on.

TONY

Well, we won't say what place you came in.

CHRYSTAL

Daddy! [Laughing] Mom always bragged about what a great father and husband you are. I think, in the present crisis, we're seeing more people ask the right questions. How do I be a better father? A better spouse?

TONY

Nothing comes before family, and if it did, your mother would be sure to let me know. A good wife is a good corrector. Like Anthony said, she used gentle strength. I had to pull back and readjust a lot.

CHRYSTAL

You championed Mom, too, and we saw that. It was all those little things, day in and day out. Mom wasn't a sports person, so you stepped up to be there at track meets and football games. Even while you were working on your master's degree, you encouraged Mom to take seminary classes and keep working on her ministry, not just be Tony Evans's wife.

I remember when we were growing up, Saturday mornings were Mom's day out. She would go grocery shopping, run errands, do some other shopping, or take the opportunity for some personal care, such as her hair or nails. You saw how hard she worked and encouraged her to take the time to refuel and refresh. But you didn't just call Mom a good wife and mother because she did all those things for us. Just as you called out spiritual gifts in us, you called out gifts in her too. You celebrated who Mom was as a person.

TONY

I was happy to do that. It was my privilege. It was the gift and blessing of my life to be able to do that for your mom.

The look on Mommy's face says it all.

CHRYSTAL

I remember the day in college when I had to tell you and Mom that I was pregnant. I know you had high hopes for all of your kids, but I was the firstborn. I know that had to hurt.

TONY

Obviously, we were disappointed. Personally, parentally, ministerially. But you are my daughter. I can't stop loving you. We wanted to see you healed spiritually because, first of all, it was a spiritual issue. We could surround you and see God take this situation and intervene in it, which He has graciously and gratefully done.

> **The great thing about the Lord is when we come back to Him, He can take the messes we have made of our lives and still lay out a beautiful miracle.**

God took disappointment and turned it into restoration. The great thing about the Lord is when we come back to Him, He can take the messes we have made of our lives and still lay out a beautiful miracle. We love the Lord, and our desire was to love you back to Him and back to a wholesome future.

CHRYSTAL

You asked me, "Is there anything we did that helped cause this situation? Anything we can change?" That question took me off guard. You didn't come at me with anger or blaming. You asked how you could serve me better. You did not focus on what I did but on what you could change. I knew I didn't have to carry the burden alone. You were like, "Here I am. I'm looking at my behavior too." To me, that's a father's heart—I am here to help you and love you back home, whatever it takes.

What were you like as a kid in school?

TONY

I wasn't academically inclined at all. That didn't come until college. As a kid, it was all sports. Football in the fall, swimming through the winter, and baseball in the spring. My whole life was church and sports.

CHRYSTAL

You talk about pressing in closer to the Lord lately. What's He been saying to you?

TONY

This is a season of drawing near to God. At seventy years old, you know the years ahead of you are a lot less than what is behind. I'm not as focused on accomplishing great things in ministry as much as seeking relational intimacy. That is where I feel called right now. Draw close to God. That's how I want to finish. But as long as there is a vision, I will keep carrying on.

CHRYSTAL

A worldwide pandemic, earthquakes, civil and political unrest, wars, rumors of wars, hurricanes hitting like never before. Do you think we are in the end times?

TONY

The introduction of the end times is very possible. Or maybe this is a cultural reset. The world has gotten so far from God that He's allowed these calamities to interrupt the world and get our attention. But, perhaps what's most important, this is something to wake up the church. In Acts 8, God allowed trouble to come to the church because they had become too comfortable. The church today is too complacent, and now it's time for a wake-up call. God does not skip the church house to fix the White House.

CHRYSTAL

Thanks for joining me for morning coffee, Daddy. That's all for now but *you know*, I'll call you later when I come up with some more questions to ask you.

TONY

[Laughing] And you know that *I know* you will!

Grandchildren and Great-Grandchildren: Kingdom Legacy

THIRTEEN

STRENGTH IN YOUR STRUGGLES

> The LORD is the everlasting God,
> the Creator of the whole earth.
> He never becomes faint or weary;
> there is no limit to his understanding.
> He gives strength to the faint
> and strengthens the powerless.
> Youths may become faint and weary,
> and young men stumble and fall,
> but those who trust in the LORD
> will renew their strength;
> they will soar on wings like eagles;
> they will run and not become weary,
> they will walk and not faint.
> —ISAIAH 40:28–31

TONY

Recently, one of my granddaughters quit eating for four straight days. Her parents tried to persuade her with several of her favorite foods, but nothing seemed to work, and they were getting more worried as the time passed.

"What is wrong?" they begged. "Why won't you eat?"

Finally, she responded in a low, sad voice. "I just don't know what's happening to our family."

It was clear. All of the loss and heartache we'd been facing was taking a toll on even the youngest members of our family.

JONATHAN

At first, it was difficult trying to figure out why my oldest daughter, Kelsey, a vibrant, healthy ten-year-old, didn't have an appetite for several days. But once we figured out why she wasn't eating, it was even harder. How do you help a child process the deaths of so many people she loves? You can't exactly say, "Well, Kelsey, our family is under spiritual attack."

It's a heartbreaking thing to hear your child say, "Daddy, is something gonna happen to me next?" Indeed, for our family, this has been the most difficult time of our lives.

TONY

I lost my brother, my sister, my brother-in-law, my niece, my father at Thanksgiving, and my wife just after Christmas. Priscilla had half of a lung removed because of a cancerous tumor. Then Chrystal discovered a suspicious growth too. After that, we faced the biggest pandemic in over a century, throwing our church into lockdown, halting our outreach and travel for ministry.

So many tears, so many unanswered questions. In the words of Marvin Gaye, "What's goin' on?" I'm sure you know what it's like to face one crisis after another, to struggle with confusion and pain. When it rains, it pours. Life has a way of throwing curveballs, and sometimes you get hit by the pitch.

In the book of Isaiah, God's people were struggling with multiple afflictions as they were being held captive in the pagan city of Babylon. In chapter 40, verse 27, the people cried out, "My way is hidden from the LORD, and the justice due me escapes the notice of God" (NKJV).

"What's goin' on?" God's people asked. "Don't You see our pain? If so, why would You let this happen? This isn't fair. How long, O Lord? Where are You?"

Truth is, there are times in life when God seems nowhere to be found. We feel distant, lost, forgotten. Every honest believer, at some point, comes to a place where instead of singing praises, they sing the blues. We have all cried out in the dark, "God, where are You?"

When God finally addressed His children in Isaiah 40:28, He did not speak scientifically, technologically, academically, or philosophically. "Do you not know? Have you not heard?" He asked, "The LORD is the everlasting God, the Creator of the ends of the earth. He will not grow tired or weary, and his understanding no one can fathom" (NIV).

> Every honest believer, at some point, comes to a place where instead of singing praises, they sing the blues. We have all cried out in the dark, "God, where are You?"

No one.

Not fully.

I have devoted my life to study and prayer. Let me share a hard truth I have discovered along the way: God can be difficult to understand. His ways do not always make sense to mortal men. Sometimes He will explain, but often He does not. We can ask God questions, but we cannot question God.

Asking a question is something like, "God, would You please help me to understand this situation? Can You show me some kind of purpose or good that can come out of this pain?" But to question God is to challenge His authority. Honest questions come from a place of humility; challenge is steeped in rebellion and arrogance. Challenge demands an answer. Growing up, my children could ask me any question, but I would not tolerate them challenging me. There is a difference.

I admit, I've had a lot of questions for the Lord these last few years. Faith does not exclude me from struggle. I wake up in the middle of the night. Sometimes I break down in tears several times throughout the day. I see an old photograph, and it hurts me. I hear a song that reminds me of all I have lost. I have wrestled with God and asked those same questions as His children in Babylon: Lord, have You forgotten me? Do You see what is going on here?

There have been times when I had to back up because I drifted from asking questions to questioning. During these trials, I have looked to Isaiah chapter 40 over and over again for guidance and consolation. "It is He who sits above the circle of the earth, and its inhabitants are like grasshoppers. He stretches out the heavens like a curtain, and spreads them like a tent to dwell in," Isaiah said. "Lift up your eyes and look to the heavens. To whom shall we compare Him?"

God is all-knowing, all-seeing, all-powerful, unrestricted by time and space. He is over the earth, not in it. The Lord created each star, and though there are trillions of galaxies containing an immeasurable number of stars, He knows each one by name. God is limitless yet intimate.

But the stars do not dictate our future, as astrology suggests. That's idolatry. The answer is not around us. We must look to the Creator of the stars. A low view of God in crisis means the crisis can own you. A high view of God says the crisis no longer has the last word. I cannot deny the circumstances, but I can refuse to give circumstances the final say.

Those who wait for the LORD will renew their strength, Isaiah 40:31

tells us. Waiting is a theme throughout the Bible, from Genesis to Revelation. Sarah had to wait for a baby. Noah waited for the flood. Joseph spent years waiting in prison. Jesus waited thirty years for His ministry to begin. Martha and Mary waited for resurrection. And the disciples had to wait for the Holy Spirit. Even as I write these words, we eagerly await the return of Christ.

Waiting is difficult business. Make me work, but please do not make me wait. But waiting, as described in the Bible, is a different process than what we think. The Hebrew word for "wait" is *quavah*, which means to plait, like the intertwining of hair or a rope. Waiting on the Lord is not a passive thing. It means to intertwine our lives with Him. Every circumstance, every decision, every facet of our life becomes wrapped so tightly together with the Lord that we are one.

> A high view of God says the crisis no longer has the last word. I cannot deny the circumstances, but I can refuse to give circumstances the final say.

Crisis makes you want to climb into the bed and hide. Crisis hangs over you, waking you up in the middle of the night, stealing your strength, making it hard to rest, work, play, or pray. When crisis has knocked you down and you're fighting for the next breath, a few praise songs and a Sunday-morning sermon aren't enough. You have to press in tight, walking so close with God that every breath is prayer and praise, sunrise to sunset, all through the night, weaving Jesus into every piece and portion of your life. That is the kind of waiting that brings new strength.

How can we know we are on the right track? When the majority of our time waiting on God is spent in worship and thanks instead of complaining. The Lord doesn't promise to answer every question. He doesn't promise to explain. But He does promise this in Psalm 22:3: *God inhabits the praises of His people.* And back to Isaiah 40:

Those who wait for the Lord will gain new strength . . .

1. **"THEY WILL SOAR ON WINGS LIKE EAGLES."** When a mama eagle kicks her baby out of the nest, she's trying to teach it to fly. This rarely works the first time. The eaglet flails and flaps and falls until the mama eagle swoops down to catch her baby and bring it back to the nest. One way God gives us new strength is by diving down into our situation and lifting us out of it.

2. **"THEY WILL RUN AND NOT BECOME WEARY."** Sometimes God doesn't swoop from the sky to lift us out of trouble; He gives us a second wind to run through it. I don't know about you, but when I'm running on the treadmill, I've got to have something to focus on other than the fight. My go-to is TV news. That way I'm not focused on how much time is left or how hard it is to breathe. God says that if we focus on Him, even though we're running, He will give us a second wind so we can go farther through this pain and this problem than we ever thought possible before.

3. **"THEY WILL WALK AND NOT FAINT."** When you can no longer run, start walking. Limp if you have to. Crawl even. Just keep moving forward. Life had worn me down, and I could not go one step farther, but somehow I did. I don't know *how* I got through some of these trials, but I made it. I didn't always run with confidence. Some days it might have looked like I was barely moving at all. But I pressed on because a strength greater than my own helped me to keep going.

God doesn't always fix our problems, but He will change the environment. He will send someone to give you an encouraging word. He'll bring a song to inspire you or a sermon that pierces your heart and renews hope, as if the preacher was reading your mind. And sometimes the Lord gives us the strength and grace to accept the things He will not change.

I would love to tell you that God always swoops down to rescue us from every struggle, but that isn't true. He does, however, promise to be with us in our troubles. So don't give up. Catastrophe is the time to run into God's arms, not away from them.

Those are not just words from a preacher in the pulpit. They are from me—a man who became an orphan and a widower in the same year. Each day I wait upon the Lord for new strength, trusting in His mercy, weaving the pieces of my life together with Him. Sometimes I get tired and all I can bring myself to do is walk. But as long as He walks with me, I will not faint. I will trust Him for new strength to carry on, fulfill the call, finish well, and meet Jesus in the place where there is no more loss, no more struggle, no more tears.

> **Catastrophe is the time to run into God's arms, not away from them.**

FOURTEEN

FAITH OVER FEAR

When you pass through the waters,
    I will be with you;
and when you pass through the rivers,
    they will not sweep over you.
When you walk through the fire,
    you will not be burned;
    the flames will not set you ablaze.
For I am the LORD your God,
    the Holy One of Israel, your Savior.
        —ISAIAH 43:2–3 NIV

ANTHONY

Earlier, Chrystal mentioned wrestling with God during all this upheaval and trauma. That's a good way to describe it, except for me, even though time passed and God loosened up on the headlock, sometimes I still feel trapped. It's not so easy for me to decide to choose faith over emotion. As Priscilla says, pain has a megaphone. Fear, anger, resentment—those are all forms of pain, and it can be difficult to hear the still, small voice. When the industry shuts down and work is scarce. When everything is harder than ever before. When your family has been hit by a string of medical disasters, and you feel run-down and achy as a killer virus sweeps the world. When you wonder if you're next on the Enemy's hit list. When you reach for the phone to call your mom and realize she is not here. Some days it seems like my pain has a microphone and thousand-watt PA system.

Dad always reminded us that emotion has to be the caboose rather than the engine. In other words, emotion must follow faith; we cannot be led by our feelings. But railroad cars are heavy, and the track is fixed. What I am saying is that we can know the right actions and attitudes, but putting them into practice is a totally different thing. It has been a hard season for me. Very hard.

Ministry has taken me all over the world, to all kinds of people. And God has shown me this: I am not the only one who struggles with my emotions. One of the things that helps is to talk about it.

> Dad always reminded us that emotion has to be the caboose rather than the engine. In other words, emotion must follow faith; we cannot be led by our feelings.

That's why I see a counselor. There is nothing wrong with Jesus and a therapist. I believe that with all of my heart. Some people may say, "All you need is prayer." The Bible says faith without works is dead. Work requires tools. Good therapists give us some tools for living. Good tools are simply biblical principles put into action. All truth belongs to God. Let me add this: seek out the most experienced and competent licensed therapist you can find. If they happen to work in a faith-based counseling center, that's great. But look for a quality connection and empathy first. Then go in with no filter—let it all hang out. Trust your story to a good guide.

We all need help. Some of us more than others, and there is no shame in the asking. There is no shame in taking care of yourself either, especially after you have been through a war. Grief is a bear. Fear is a grizzly. You don't want to fight bears with a flyswatter, right?

I am a perfectionist. I want everything to be right all the time, including myself. With the support of a therapist, I came to this conclusion: you have to allow yourself to be human. Not every day is going to be great. You are not going to be able to cling perfectly to all of God's promises all day, every day. That's not real, and it's not true. Not even for a family like ours. Just because I am Tony Evans Jr. does not mean I have to have it all together all the time. Dad doesn't have it all together all the time either. If humans had the ability to get themselves together and right, God could have avoided the cross.

Honesty helps in repositioning faith before fear. Humility too. Denying feelings doesn't get anybody closer to God. Like He doesn't already know?

So if I am fearful, I'm going to let that feeling come. If I'm angry, I'm going to deal with it for what it is instead of pushing it down and trying to act like everything is okay. I go through the process without numbing the pain with distraction or substances or religious display. No shortcuts. Walk through it. That's how I return to a place of joy.

Injuries take time to heal. We require help from doctors and physical therapists to get healthy and active again. That means I had to slow down and move back to a calmer pace of life. Hollywood is a one-hundred-miles-per-hour speed zone, like some crazy NASCAR circuit. I needed a pit stop to refuel before getting back on track again. I guess God figured the whole world needed a pit stop in 2020.

I've still got a long way to go, but things are better than they used to be. I realize that I have a choice. I have to own my emotions, rein them in. Emotions can be like wild horses. Untamed, they can hurt you. But once broken, that same horse can be of great service.

Every day I have to make a decision to choose faith over fear, faith over anxiety, faith over anger and doubt. Like most things worth doing, it takes a lot of work. Getting physically fit isn't easy. It takes a lot of sweat and discomfort, and you have to be willing to get up early, lift heavy things, and make your body do what it does not want to do. Getting spiritually fit is like that too. I have to push against a great deal of resistance to stay strong. I have to sweat and work and deny the flesh.

You know what else helps? Knowing that I can talk to my dad and not have to fake it or pretend. Even though we are wired differently, I can always count on him for insight. Doing so gives me confidence that I can do the same with God.

TONY

When fear takes over the driver's seat of your life, the first thing you must decide is to let fear drive you to faith. Faith requires action. This is why 2 Corinthians 5:7 calls it walking by faith.

> **Faith requires action. This is why 2 Corinthians 5:7 calls it walking by faith.**

What steps will I take to show God I am trusting Him in spite of how I feel? The action of faith will take you in a different direction than feelings alone. If you walk in that direction long enough, emotions have to adjust. Feelings begin to follow your feet.

We express our fears to God instead of hiding them. If we deny emotions, then we are lying and avoiding reality. In 2 Chronicles 17:3–6; 18:4; and 20:3, Jehoshaphat admitted that he was very much afraid and took his fear to God. Don't be so spiritual that you avoid the truth.

ANTHONY

That was me. I was so spiritual that I was not being honest. I felt like I had to figure things out on my own before I could bring them to God. In doing so, I let fear and anxiety control my life. Fear in control will always override faith.

I'm still a work in progress, but for me, the key was starting out simply with honesty, authenticity, and vulnerability. From Moses to Paul, the Bible shows us that we must first be faithful in the small things. Stretch out your hand. Give a little flour and oil. Throw a splinter of wood in the river. Fill a jar from the well. Offer up some fish and bread. Often some seemingly insignificant act leads to the breakthrough that will renew and solidify our faith.

When the coronavirus quarantine first started, I decided to return to Dallas. I thought the lockdown would be a few weeks at most, so I rented an Airbnb to have my own space. Dad likes to keep the house hot, and there is no way I could sleep up in that. Every grown kid who has gone home for the holidays knows how the whole thing with dads and thermostats goes.

Anyway, I rented a house in a newer part of town. It's really nice, trees and sidewalks and parks. The lockdown gave us all plenty of time. Too much time, however, will drive you crazy. So one day I went out for a walk, and in this beautiful up-and-coming neighborhood there was suddenly an awful stench. Like, really bad. Like, T-shirt over your face, wish-I-had-a-mask bad. This was before masks were a thing. *Man, what stinks?*

Well, I found out. Those new trees and beautiful plants? They require fertilizer. You know what fertilizer is a fancy word for, right? In Texas, they call it some other names.

But then I realized something. That wretched smell represented new growth and development. Something beautiful was emerging from that stink. That's what it takes to be spiritually mature: the ability to look at something nasty in your life and realize that God is planting something new. The stench is just part of the process.

Illustrations help me understand God and biblical principles, so here's another story for you. When my niece Kariss was a little girl, we had a lot of dogs in our neighborhood. One day Kariss was playing on the sidewalk, and a big, mean German shepherd headed straight for her, barking and baring his teeth.

"Poppy!" she screamed, running to where my dad was standing on the porch. With a snarling dog hot on her heels, Dad scooped Kariss into his arms and lifted her up out of harm's way. She looked down at the angry dog, and then looked back at Dad. The crying stopped, and confidence took over. "Nanny, nanny, boo-boo," Kariss said, taunting the dog.

The circumstances did not change, but her perspective did. She was safe in the arms of her grandfather.

We had a two-year period of devastating loss followed by a pandemic that completely turned our lives, careers, and ministries upside down. That forced me to change my perspective. When you hold your mother's hand as she takes her final breath, that hurts. But even in the ugliest, most difficult moments of life, even when my emotions were stomping me into the dirt, I could realize that God was doing something new.

> God says that no matter where we are in life, no matter what we have been through, we can always start over again. He brings beauty from ashes, joy from pain, faith from our deepest fears.

In fact, you are holding the evidence of that in your hands right now. This book was born from the pain and struggle of that season. Me, Dad, and my siblings, all of us together here, telling our stories about pain and growth and change in a whole new way. Talking about humility and grace and starting over again. About just how much we need each other.

Not just my family and me. All of us. God's people. Whosoever will. We help each other down here. God says that no matter where we are in life, no matter what we have been through, we can always start over again. He brings beauty from ashes, joy from pain, faith from our deepest fears.

I am still in my Airbnb. That thirty-day lockdown has lasted all the way through spring, summer, fall, and winter. Now, it's spring again. I still go for walks and I see those big planters. But I don't smell the stench anymore. Everywhere I look, there is new growth and new life. Romans 8:28 tells us, "All things work together for the good of those who love God, who are called according to his purpose."

Here we are. All of us together. Trusting God.

FIFTEEN

THE RIGHT THING ALONG THE WAY

If you follow my statutes and faithfully observe my commands, I will give you rain at the right time, and the land will yield its produce, and the trees of the field will bear their fruit. Your threshing will continue until grape harvest, and the grape harvest will continue until sowing time; you will have plenty of food to eat and live securely in your land. I will give peace to the land, and you will lie down with nothing to frighten you. . . . I will turn to you, make you fruitful and multiply you, and confirm my covenant with you. . . . I will place my residence among you, and I will not reject you. I will walk among you and be your God, and you will be my people.

—LEVITICUS 26:3–6, 9, 11–12

PRISCILLA

How awesome is it that *The Karate Kid* made a comeback in the twenty-first century as *Cobra Kai*? I was a kid when the original trilogy came out in the eighties, so it's cool to watch Daniel LaRusso and Johnny Lawrence work out their issues as adults. The updated show is somehow both nostalgic and new and, like before, the story contains a lot of important life lessons: patience, humility, persistence, and compassion, even for one's enemies. Powerful film and television shows can be incredible parables, showing us the lesson instead of delivering it as a lecture. In story form, important principles can often slip past the mind and embed themselves in the soul. Like an important one that I learned from Mr. Miyagi in *The Karate Kid*.

The kindhearted sensei is training young Daniel-san, but Daniel doesn't realize he is being trained. He believes Miyagi is just giving him menial tasks to do around the dojo.

"Wax my collection of antique cars."

"Sand the floor."

"Paint the fence, up and down strokes. Both side!"

"Now, paint the house, different stroke, side to side motions now."

Daniel becomes frustrated and certain that Mr. Miyagi is using him for nothing more than to do maintenance work around his property instead of teaching him the discipline of martial arts. Until one day when Mr. Miyagi prophesies, "Not everything is as it seems. Show me wax on, wax off."

Daniel mimics the circular motion of applying wax to a car's fender. Suddenly, Mr. Miyagi throws a punch that Daniel-san can intuitively block. "Now," Miyagi says. "Paint the fence."

Another quick jab. Another block from Daniel. "Sand the floor," the old master commands. As Miyagi throws kicks, Daniel deflects each one.

The Bible tells us in Luke 16:10, "If you are faithful in the small things, you will be faithful in that which is great."

Daniel did not enjoy the repetition of those seemingly unrelated tasks. Little did he know that the master was training him for battle all along.

I believe that principle applies to our lives as well. We wash clothes and dishes, fix leaking faucets, change diapers, cut grass, clean countertops, cook meals, file papers, and prepare for meetings. We deal with traffic jams and difficult people, sometimes within our own families. Most days it feels as if we are just going through the motions, doing the maintenance of life, wondering when we will find our purpose and really start living, doing great things for God.

While it feels as though the Master is training us in things that seem insignificant, He is actually training our character, shaping our reflexes, showing us actions and attitudes that are going to keep us steady and stable for what's coming next. None of our actions are in vain or without holy intent. As we are faithful in the small tasks—in action and attitude—the disciplines of everyday life become the training ground for victory in the future.

My mother received her doctorate and became an accomplished leader, speaker, mentor, and author of several books. You know what she did before all of that, back when Oak Cliff Bible Fellowship first began? She typed bulletins, played piano for worship, and took care of the church's kids. Whatever needed to be done, Mom did it. Every task she did *then* prepared her and my Dad to lead the church with integrity and excellence as it grew to astounding numbers. It prepared them to handle the weight of an international radio-and-television ministry with dignity and grace.

Along the way, Mom committed to keep a private journal to chronicle what the Lord was doing in her life. She wrote about hard things, discouraging things, and also those things that gave her joy and fulfillment. She didn't write daily, but she wrote consistently. Mom had no way of knowing those entries would become source material for the chapters of the books she would write decades later to encourage thousands of believers worldwide.

Consistency is the key. Wax on, wax off.

God prepares us through the ordinary, everyday tasks of life. There are no insignificant tasks in God's kingdom.

Life throws punches, most of them unexpected, but God prepares us through the ordinary, everyday tasks of life. There are no insignificant tasks in God's kingdom. Whether you are preaching to ten thousand or tying a five-year-old's shoes.

CHRYSTAL

It doesn't take some great psychologist to connect a messed-up, broken life with major heartbreaking and destructive decisions made along the way. Those dots are usually pretty easy to connect. But I believe our position in life is largely determined by the small choices we make day in and day out. And those nuances are not always so easy to see.

I see those life decisions in the 2016 movie *Hidden Figures*. In this amazing film, the smallest calculations by NASA mathematician Katherine Johnson made the biggest impact and were the determining factor between a perfect landing and a fiery crash. Most of us don't struggle with the temptation to rob a convenience store. But what about the little decisions we make throughout each day, whether doing personal business on company time or fudging the truth to get out of some function you'd rather not attend? Turning in careless work, skipping your morning quiet time with God, parking your kids in front of the Disney Channel instead of pressing in and taking an active role in their development?

The way we act on an everyday basis? That's our walk with God. There is an old proverb: "I practice daily what I believe. Everything else is just religious talk." The choices we make determine our legacy, the difference between a life of restless confusion and a life lived well for others and God.

People often ask my parents how they managed to raise four children who love Jesus and are faithful to God's house. I think they are looking for some secret trick or magical piece of advice. There is no secret. Mom and Dad showed us firsthand what a life of integrity looks like. They didn't praise the Lord from the front pew and then present a totally different way at home. They both lived lives on Monday that were consistent with what we saw on Sunday. Consistency matters, because, let me tell you, your kids are watching every move. We sure were.

I saw the small decisions my parents made every day. "As for me and my house, we will serve the LORD" was not just a plaque on our living room wall. Mom and Dad made choices every day that proved God was in charge of our lives. We sat down together for meals, and it was strictly family time. We prayed before school. We spent time together playing games, having family talent shows, and diving into family discussions. We were together a whole bunch—even when we couldn't stand each other. We were a family, but brothers and sisters aren't always excited to be family when they are growing up together.

I now know that my parents did not always feel like organizing family time. I know there were days when Dad was frazzled from flying all over the country to preach and just wanted to sit in his chair and watch the ball game without being interrupted or maybe even take a nap. I'm sure that Mom got sick of cooking dinner and cleaning the kitchen or making sure we did our job when it was our turn to help. But my parents made a decision that the Evans family would live a life that honored God, and they were determined to walk it out in all the small things, day by day, together.

That's Kingdom Legacy.

It's all about small everyday decisions. How do you treat your next-door neighbor during a pandemic? That's legacy.

> **My parents made a decision that the Evans family would live a life that honored God, and they were determined to walk it out in all the small things, day by day, together.**
> **That's Kingdom Legacy.**

Who are you when the schools shut down and your kids are underfoot every minute of every day? That is your legacy. How do you act when money gets tight and you have to make some difficult decisions?

I realize that all along the way I've been practicing who I would become. I have been working on me the whole time, through both good and bad decisions, and with the way I handled success or setbacks. The blessing of the small, everyday decision is that you don't have to wait for major moments to change. You can simply start where you are and move forward doing the next right thing.

Lamentations 3:3 says that His mercies are new every morning. Each day is a chance to start over and experience the blessings of what it means to be God's child. No matter who you are or where you are, you can always start making better choices. And no matter what you have done or how many mistakes you've made along the way, God always offers us the grace to start again.

ANTHONY

That was an incredible word from my oldest sister, so I need to take the opportunity to do the right thing along the way right now. When we were growing up, Chrystal was so slow to come to conclusions, it used to drive me crazy. Sometimes it drove me crazy even after we were grown. Patience was never something that came easy for me, and often I would push her buttons to try and spur her into action.

But just in these last few years, especially during the writing of this book, I have learned that you've got to let Chrystal be Chrystal in her own time. Pressure does not work. If I just back up, give her space, and let her collect her thoughts, she will come through and hit the shot every time.

"Be completely humble and patient," Ephesians 4:2 tells us, "bearing with one another in love." If going through hard times teaches us anything, it should be grace.

I received a valuable lesson in doing the right thing along the way pretty early into my music career. When I first started out, I had a difficult time finding a place where I fit in. The Christian music industry leaders in Nashville told me I was too contemporary for gospel and too gospel for contemporary. The bottom line was I was not as marketable as they initially thought, so they did not know what to do with me.

For a while I tried various things to please people, trying to prove that I was a team player. I strapped on a guitar even though I didn't know how to play it. I changed up my sound and recorded songs I didn't like. I even changed my clothes in an attempt to appeal to the contemporary Christian crowd.

I was desperate for acceptance back in those days. Sometimes, in an effort to sell yourself, you end up selling out. A lot of those projects are embarrassing to me now, because I was trying to be something I was not. But I was younger then and I think most of us go through a phase like that.

Eventually, I had to make the decision to be in no-man's-land. Better to be in the desert with God than in a palace without Him. My music career did not really begin until I understood that the Lord had called me to a new thing and a new direction, something particularly suited for the way He made me. And for a long time I had to keep moving forward in the dark, even though I could not see the results. I had to be obedient to my specific calling and completely reliant on God.

Most of that was figuring it out as I went along. Kind of like Moses in the desert, it takes a bit of wandering. Having a vision helps with the discipline of those daily choices, but often God only reveals enough for us to take the next step. I became my own manager and booking agent, reaching out to churches and special events to let them know I was available to come and minister. I had to leave the security of a record label and start doing projects on my own, with my own music.

Stepping out in faith to do music and ministry that fit me took a lot of small, difficult decisions every day. But days add up to weeks and weeks turn into months, and eventually a pattern begins to form. Obedience plus persistence brings change. I didn't realize at the time that God was preparing me to have my own ministry and production company. In fact, this book came together under the umbrella of Sherman James Productions. I named the company after my two grandfathers: Arthur Sherman "Two Daddy" Evans and James Cannings. Their dedication to excellence in work and faith caused a ripple effect that is still being felt by our family to this day. Thank God for their commitment to pursue courage and faith over comfort.

When we do the right thing along the way, we blaze new trails, not only for ourselves, but for the next generation as well.

--- SIXTEEN ---

DWELL

He who dwells in the secret place of the Most High
Shall abide under the shadow of the Almighty.
I will say of the Lᴏʀᴅ, "He is my refuge and my
   fortress;
My God, in Him I will trust."

—PSALM 91:1–2 ɴᴋᴊᴠ

CHRYSTAL

Recently, a friend of mine was suffering from terrible allergies, and her doctor prescribed an elimination diet. Basically, she had to stop eating anything that might be causing her problem. Nuts, spices, shellfish, milk, eggs, caffeine, wheat, artificial sweeteners, soy. It got to where she was pretty much living on vegetables, water, and bananas. Little by little, she added things back into her diet until she figured out what was making her sick. (It was wheat.)

If you've ever struggled with sickness in your body, you know that sometimes the only way to move forward and get back to a good quality of life is by cutting out those things that are hurting you. And not just by changing your diet or having something surgically removed, but by cutting out bad habits or lifestyle choices that are making you sick.

God made all things to work together for the good physically, spiritually, and mentally. But sometimes, in order to prioritize our spiritual health, we need to pull away from anything that might be holding us back. Not even things that are necessarily sinful. Maybe too much television or video games is getting in the way of connection with God. Maybe you are avoiding the difficulties of life by overeating or working too much. Maybe you do more than is balanced when you compare your religious activities to time you spend with God. None of those things are inherently evil, but the Bible tells us that anything that holds us back from God can become an idol and get more of our focus or energy than is right.

> Sometimes, in order to prioritize our spiritual health, we need to pull away from anything that might be holding us back.

God commands that we devote our heart, mind, and soul to Him. He is a loving but jealous God. So if we are watching five hours of Netflix a night, but we cannot spend five minutes in prayer and the Word, it's time for an elimination diet. Cut it all back. Remove anything from your life that may be distracting you from God.

We are living in a season when the state of the world has removed a lot of our distractions because of the pandemic. Like it or not, we have been pushed toward a more restrictive lifestyle that is in some ways simpler than many of us have ever known. There is less rush, less traffic, very few social engagements, and a lot more unstructured time in each day. I am not suggesting the pandemic is a big blessing of simplicity. But there is a lot more opportunity to spend time with God these days. And there is the need. Because in forced rest there is also anxiety and fear.

Scripture tells us the solution for fear and anxiety is to draw close to the Lord. To abide in Him and rest in the shadow of His wing, to let our praise and fellowship be unbroken. When the storm hits, anxious sheep stay close to the shepherd's side.

Now is the time to dwell.

- When too many loved ones pass away in a short period of time, *press into the Lord.*
- When you walk through the valley of the shadow of death as a virus sweeps the planet, *draw near to God.*
- When the streets are filled with violence and unrest and grocery store shelves are empty and hospitals are full, *cling to hope in Jesus.*

This is a time for more prayer, more devotion, more worship, more time in the Word. Our strength is found in the joy of the Lord. "Dwell" simply means that we remain in a constant state of fellowship with our Father, putting aside everything that might distract us from His purpose and running our race to win.

ANTHONY

My father always wanted us to be ahead of where people expected us to be, to rise above, pursue excellence, and go the extra mile. So one day he sat us all down to talk about the principles of investing.

"Leave your resources in something you believe in," Dad told us. "Don't jump in and out. Whether it is a stock or a company, leave it there and let it grow."

I believe that dwelling is putting an investment into the Word of God. We place our hope and trust there, and then leave it and watch that investment grow over time. That takes persistence and a lot of patience. It's tempting to jump in and out and look for faster ways to get ahead, but the Bible tells us that double-minded people are unstable in all of their ways. Leave it there. Continue to invest. Believe that God's promises are true. Believe that His kingdom and His will be done on earth just as it is in heaven.

Back in normal, pre-COVID times—which seems like ten years ago now—some friends took me off the California coast in a big boat. I'm amazed by how things work, so they showed me the engine room. When a storm hits, the navigation system kicks in, and powerful jets autocorrect the balance so the boat won't crash or get lost at sea. I thought that was a pretty good illustration for faith and staying close to God.

Storms will come. But if you have a solid foundation of faith, then the stabilizers can kick in. A Bible verse comes to mind, you pray or reach out to someone for help. The autopilot may not always take you out of the storm, but it will help you stay upright and not get lost.

PRISCILLA

My mother's favorite Bible verse was John 15:1–5, 8:

> I am the true vine, and My Father is the vineyard keeper. Every branch in Me that does not produce fruit He removes, and He prunes every branch that produces fruit so that it will produce more fruit. You are already clean because of the word I have spoken to you. Remain in Me, and I in you. Just as a branch is unable to produce fruit by itself unless it remains on the vine, so neither can you unless you remain in Me. I am the vine; you are the branches. The one who remains in Me and I in him produces much fruit, because you can do nothing without Me. . . . My Father is glorified by this: that you produce much fruit and prove to be My disciples.

In these verses Jesus discussed the principle of abiding. He put it in the context of gardening and talked about the Father as the vinedresser. He is the true vine, He said, but we are the branches.

Notice in Jesus' illustration only two players actually do the work. The vinedresser actively takes care of the vines, and the vines pump nutrients into the branches and make sure that each of them is well sustained. The only component of this illustration that does more resting than working is the branch.

Verse 5 says, "You are the branches."

If we want to produce fruit, we don't have to strive for it. We don't have to sweat or lose sleep or grit our teeth in anxiety to achieve it. The branch's only responsibility is to remain connected to and to rest in the vine, to ensure the connection is not superficial but deeply intertwined below the surface. Intimate connection is the only way the branch will receive the nutrition needed to thrive. To truly flourish, the branch must stay deeply rooted in the vine.

This is the concept of abiding, concentrating on maintaining a fervent and vibrant connection with God throughout the regular rhythms of the day. I believe that looks less like a Sunday-morning church experience or even a daily quiet time. Those things are important, but abiding is more like what Brother Lawrence described as "practicing the presence of God."

Brother Lawrence was a seventeenth-century Carmelite monk in Paris who made sandals for a living. We don't know much more about Brother Lawrence because he never sought recognition. His only goals in life were to serve and seek God and to cultivate a lively friendship with the Lord that lasted all day, every day.

An older woman in the faith once directed me to Brother Lawrence's book on intimacy with Jesus and gave me this piece of advice: "Write down one or two verses of Scripture on several three-by-five cards, and put them in the places where you spend your time. Tape one to the dashboard of your car, another over the kitchen sink, one on the bathroom mirror. This way, you'll be running into God's Word as you go throughout your day. Meditate on what the Scriptures say. Pray about them, asking God's Spirit to speak to you and inscribe their message on your heart."

I took her suggestion and spread those cards all over my life. Everywhere I went, the Word was waiting, reminding me to stay close, providing an opportunity for constant prayer and realignment. When some trouble would pop up—and trouble will surely come—the Word was there. When difficult people crossed my path, there was a Bible verse to remind me that the most important thing I could do is keep a deep connection to the vine.

When the atmosphere around you dries up, when your health fails, when your friends betray you, when the endeavor you've worked so hard on falters, when you're not appreciated or even noticed, when the road gets tough to traverse, when loved ones die and your ministry flounders, when your heart is broken, Jesus said there is only one thing that will give you the continued sustenance and nourishment that you need to have a well of joy and hope.

Rest in Him.

Abide.

Cultivate and deepen your friendship with Jesus as a priority of life. Your strength over time and the ability to bear eternal fruit depends on it. Not just when it's trendy and cool or you're applauded and noticed. Make a decision to deepen your relationship with the Lord every day, every single week, throughout every single season, good or bad.

JONATHAN

Between the pandemic and personal losses, I've come to realize that healing comes with sitting in an open, truthful relationship with the Lord. Not out of religion or requirement or anything other than dwelling in relationship with Him every single day.

Relationship is built on honesty. Honesty about my pain, my disappointments, my expectations. Instead of pretending, I talk to God about the times I feel that He failed me or how it seemed like so many of those promises we proclaimed did not come to pass. If I feel that God has let me down, I talk to Him about it instead of hiding it. To me, that's true intimacy. I'm not acting like I'm okay and keeping it all inside because that's the proper religious thing to do.

Be real. Tell the truth. God can handle it.

And that works both ways. It's not just me unloading on God; it's God talking straight to me, reminding me who He is, even if things don't turn out the way I had hoped or planned. It's about experiencing prayer as a dialogue instead of a monologue. When life is moving fast, prayer can become a monologue. But now? I have to sit and wait for answers because I have nowhere else to go.

No clichés or churchy words or those things we feel like we're supposed to say because we think that's what God wants to hear. Second Corinthians 3:18 tells us to come to God with an unveiled face. In other words, don't put on. Be real. Tell the truth. God can handle it.

TONY

For me, the concept of dwelling and abiding has meant more time meditating on God's Word. There is less sense of urgency now, so I try to take advantage of that. Sometimes in the middle of the night when

I wake up, I pray and meditate. Most mornings, I read three chapters of the Bible. I reflect more on the things that matter, and it's been good for me to spend time with God without it being tied to a program or a sermon series. The most important thing this season has highlighted is my need for God, for His presence and guidance and help.

Moses told the Lord in Exodus 33:15, "If You don't go with us, we're not going to go." So it's not so much about goals or plans, it's about His presence. I don't want the blessing of the promised land if I can't have God too. Better to stay in the desert with God than enter the promised land without Him. Even in my own life, I had to prioritize relationship over the work.

SEVENTEEN

THE ART OF SURRENDER

Therefore, since we have been justified through faith, we
have peace with God through our Lord Jesus Christ, through
whom we have gained access by faith into this grace in which
we now stand. And we boast in the hope of the glory of God.
Not only so, but we also glory in our sufferings, because we
know that suffering produces perseverance; perseverance,
character; and character, hope. And hope does not put us
to shame, because God's love has been poured out into our
hearts through the Holy Spirit, who has been given to us.

—ROMANS 5:1–5 NIV

TONY

How could I remain hopeful after God did not answer one of the biggest prayers of my life—to heal my wife? How can I possibly continue to encourage others to hold on to hope?

Hope is our expectation for the future. I had hopes that my wife, Lois, would be completely restored. We had goals, dreams of the future, great things we wanted to do together for the Lord and with each other.

God chose not to answer my prayer in the way I had hoped. So I

> .God chose not to answer my prayer in the way I had hoped. So I had to hold on to a hope that God, in His wisdom, had a greater purpose and plan that could only be fulfilled in this way.

had to hold on to a hope that God, in His wisdom, had a greater purpose and plan that could only be fulfilled in this way. So I cling to hope in Him. Hope for strength, for courage, for help in finding a way to move forward. Hope that God can take all the pain and confusion and reveal a deeper experience of His love than ever before.

In the face of loss, we must appeal to what we know is true about God. In those dark, early-morning hours as my wife passed away, I had to let go and trust in His sovereignty and kindness. "Lord, it's not my will," I told Him, "but Your will be done." That was an act of surrender, and I won't pretend it was an easy thing to do. Every believer will face a moment when you have to yield to His final decision and say yes to God about a no He has said to you.

That is a breaking process, and it is very painful. But it is also the place where God begins a new thing. Rarely do we understand it at the time. The Lord does not ask that we be okay with being broken. He only asks that we submit to the breaking and trust Him with it. The apex of obedience to God is to faithfully say, "Lord, let this cup pass from me; nevertheless, not my will, but Your will be done," to release what is behind and press on to what lies ahead, to surrender, to let God close the door, regardless of how much it hurts.

Let Abraham testify. He was commanded to surrender his will and lay his son, Isaac, on the altar of sacrifice. Isaac was Abraham's miracle baby, born when his father was one hundred years old. And yet God called Abraham to lay his miracle on the altar at Mount Moriah. Facing the biggest loss in his life also led to Abraham's biggest miracle, becoming not just Isaac's father but the father of many nations.

Lois and I created a miracle together, just two young kids with a dream and a vision. I had to climb the mountain and lay that dream down before the Lord. The only way you can put a miracle on an altar is to understand the art of surrender. You cannot surrender to someone you do not trust. Trust enables surrender. You have to know and believe in the character of God, in His love and commitment for your best, trusting that He knows what He is doing, that He sees a far bigger picture than you can imagine.

One of the reasons we study theology is to learn about the nature of God so we can have a deeply rooted trust in Him. My biological father gave me a great example of this type of trusting relationship. I knew that he cared for me and would provide for our family's needs. I did not worry about food or clothes because I was confident my father would take care of those things.

The Evans family faced our share of difficult times. My father did not have a high school education. He was a longshoreman, unloading freight from cargo ships to the docks on the Chesapeake Bay in Baltimore. Some days there was no work to be had, but Dad was determined to do whatever he could to raise up his family and survive.

One advantage to being raised on the waterfront was that there were always fish available. Many days I came home from school to the smell of herring cooking in Mom's kitchen. Herring is basically a big sardine with lots of those nasty little bones in it, and to this day I cannot stand to eat fish of any kind. But my father honored the family table, and we always began with thanks and devotion. I trusted Dad would take care of our needs and that he was diligently working with my best interest at heart.

I've heard that fresh herring is one of the most nutritious things a person can eat, full of antioxidants and those omega-3 fatty acids that doctors say are so important. We may have grumbled about all that fish, but my siblings and I were a hearty bunch. God had a plan after all.

CHRYSTAL

My husband, Jessie, and I have five children. At one point, our oldest was taking college classes while our youngest was just starting kindergarten—and I homeschooled them all. I started out totally career-minded and corporate bound, ready to take over the world. I ended up a homeschooling, bread-baking, garden-growing, cloth-diapering mommy blogger. Isn't life crazy? But I wouldn't trade that time with my family for anything.

One of the things I've learned from teaching young children is that there are times when you cannot make progress without trust. For example, if one of my kids brings a math problem to me, we'll often do this dance where I try to teach them how to find the solution, but it seems as if they want to convince me that they know what they are doing! They don't want to rest in the fact that I already know the answer. Children do not easily surrender their will. That's human nature though. We all want to do things our own way.

At some point in the lesson, I have to lean down, eye to eye, and in a very calm and loving manner ask, "Do you want me to help you or not?"

If the reply is yes, then my child has to trust that I know what I am talking about and that there is a plan. Progress requires surrender. It involves one person allowing another to lead and show the way. Surrender invites humility and admits "I do not know."

I love the Psalms because even though God called David a man after His own heart, he obviously struggled with surrendering to God's will. David didn't sugarcoat the struggle. In one psalm he's singing "Bless the Lord, oh, my soul," and in another song he's crying and wondering if God has forgotten about him.

I can relate to that, can't you?

But at the end of the day, after King David got his emotions off his chest, he always pointed back to God as his source, his helper, and his friend. He remembers God's goodness, His presence, all the times He delivered David in his hour of need. He admitted that God knows the plan and he did not.

David coupled honesty with release. Surrendering to God doesn't mean you don't have an opinion. Trust is not some robotic response. It just means you realize that God has been doing this life thing a lot longer than you have. There is nothing new under the sun. The Lord has seen a thousand generations come and go.

First Peter 5:7 tells us to cast all of our cares upon Him, for He cares for us. That's trust. First Thessalonians 5:17–18 says to pray without ceasing and give thanks in *all* circumstances, for this is God's will. That is surrender. Even Jesus, in the garden of Gethsemane in Luke 22:39–42, prayed to not face the cross. And yet He finished his prayer with, "Not my will but thine be done." Jesus surrendered His will.

If you pay attention, lessons on surrender are everywhere. Just last week I had to go to the Apple Store. I've been using Apple products for a long time now, and I have made a few trips to ask them for help. I can tell you the whole process. In fact, I found myself overexplaining to the tech how and why and when and what the problem was with my phone. I was standing there at the counter, talking and talking, wheels spinning while the blue-shirted Apple guy's eyes started to glaze over.

That's when it hit me. I was just like my children when I'm trying to teach them something. Did I want help or not? Was I really standing at the Genius Bar and acting like I had it all figured out? Because, obviously, I didn't, or I would have been able to fix my phone on my own. The best thing I could do was stop talking and admit I didn't have all the answers. Please help me. I am lost.

But that takes humility. And humility, for all of us, is a very, very difficult thing.

Trust and surrender are realizing we are like a seven-year-old child

> Surrender is admitting that God's plan is better.

trying to grasp long division. There are things in life we do not have the capacity to understand. And so we must place our trust in a power and a knowledge far bigger than our own.

Surrender is admitting that God's plan is better. Sometimes that's easy to admit and yield to, but surrender requires faith.

EIGHTEEN

DIVINE RESET

In his kindness God called you to share in his eternal
glory by means of Christ Jesus. So after you have suffered
a little while, he will restore, support, and strengthen
you, and he will place you on a firm foundation.
—1 PETER 5:10 NLT

TONY

I realize we normally don't open a chapter with prayer, but this is an unusual kind of book for an uncommon time. You don't have to bow your head or close your eyes, but would you please pray with me, in your heart, before we move on?

Lord, thank You for the privilege of coming into Your presence.
Remove anything that would hinder me from hearing Your
voice and knowing Your thoughts toward me. Teach me,
correct me, convict me, reset me. In Jesus' name, amen.

A few years back, Lois and I remodeled our kitchen, and let me tell you, it was a hot mess. It wasn't like my fellow Texan friends on *Fixer*

Upper, where Chip Gaines makes demolition look like fun, Joanna dazzles with her gifts of style and grace, and through the magic of TV editing, a hot mess is transformed into a glorious reveal in less than an hour.

For weeks our kitchen was a disaster from ceiling to floor. Cabinets torn out, stove in the hall, no fridge, holes in every wall. You realize how much family life revolves around your kitchen *after* you wreck it. Things got so bad that we had to move in with Chrystal and Jessie for a while.

Renovation is not just laying down new tile and installing a deeper sink. The goal of remodeling is to build back better than before. We were fed up with our old, outdated, poorly functioning kitchen. If you really want to do your remodel right, you've got to tear that space down to the wires and pipes and start back fresh.

I believe this world is under a major renovation right now. The Lord has allowed us to experience divine disruption to prepare for a divine reset. There is a purpose behind the problem. God is shaking the earth to reveal heaven.

When the Lord disturbs something, it serves to highlight the spiritual over the physical. Discomfort gets our attention, but it's the underlying issues that are at the heart of change. We have allowed our spiritual lives to fracture and go stale, going through the motions of Bible study and prayer. When our efforts are mostly surface, God becomes an afterthought.

The Bible is clear that there will be a global shake-up before Christ comes for the ultimate restoration of this broken world. Jesus turned things upside down two thousand years ago, and soon, very soon, He is going to do it again.

In Luke 5 Jesus called His disciples to leave their old lives behind and follow Him. Levi, also known as Matthew, threw a big party for the Lord. Listen, Jesus didn't mind a party. He was not opposed to good times, good food, and good fellowship. But this was not the standard church social. An interesting group attended Jesus' party. The Bible calls them tax collectors and sinners. Levi was a tax collector. Maybe his old coworkers? Some of Peter's roughneck friends from the fishing docks?

The Pharisees found out there was a party going on, so they showed up to see that Jesus was running with a rough crowd. Never ones to miss a platform, the religious leaders sought to prove their spiritual superiority by setting Jesus straight.

In verse 30 they asked, "Why do you eat and drink [and hang out] with tax collectors and sinners?"

The Pharisees had two problems. First on the list was a seemingly inappropriate party for Rabbi Jesus. Second, they weren't even the main ones invited. Jesus' party was filled with the kind of rank sinners who cursed, drank, and laughed too loud; loose women; tax cheats; and blue-collar workers who were too tired to pretend. The Pharisees didn't have time for people like this.

Jesus not only tolerated this crowd, He seemed to enjoy their company and vice versa. They ate and drank together, maybe cracked some jokes. This Rabbi Jesus was a heretic. He had the nerve to fellowship with reprobates.

"It is not those who are healthy who need a doctor," Jesus responded to the Pharisees, "but those who are sick. I have not come to call the righteous, but sinners to repentance."

Well, the Pharisees didn't like this reply one bit. In verse 33 they fired back, "John's disciples fast often and say prayers. And those of the Pharisees do the same, but yours eat and drink."

Fasting is forsaking the flesh to accentuate the spiritual. I'm all for it. Our church does a fast every year. But did you know there was only one required fast in the Bible? Leviticus 16 describes Yom Kippur, the Day of Atonement. In order for God's people to get right with God, there was a call to fast. Every other biblical fast was voluntary due to crisis or grief, anything that needed the presence of God.

False religion is adding man-made rules to God's Word, and the Pharisees had turned fasting into a twice-a-week requirement. In 2 Timothy 3:5, Paul called this having a "form of godliness but denying its power."

Jesus refused to play the Pharisees' game. He did not care what the religious big shots had to say or some new guidelines the denomination handed down. Jesus disrupted things. He went to parties and changed water into wine, broke Sabbath laws to heal the sick, turned over the money-changing tables in the church foyer and chased out the thieves with a whip! Jesus brought disruption so restoration could take place.

We all have to be cautious of ritual at the expense of relationship, going through some spiritual motions to get brownie points with God.

> We all have to be cautious of ritual at the expense of relationship, going through some spiritual motions to get brownie points with God.

Some people make external gestures that seem spiritual, Jesus warned, "but in truth, their hearts are far from Him." Religion makes good camouflage to fool the neighbors and hide from God. It may sound harsh, but the Lord often has to demolish our reality in order to bring change.

I'm not suggesting God unleashed a plague to teach us a lesson, but in the broad sense I feel He has said, "I'm closing the church doors for a while. I am going to change the paradigm. I'm not going to let you do things like you used to do because you have valued religion over relationship with Me. So let's tear it down to the foundation and start over again."

Jesus shared two illustrations on that theme in Luke 5:36–38: "No one tears a patch from a new garment and puts it on an old garment. Otherwise, not only will he tear the new, but also the piece from the new garment will not match the old. And no one puts new wine into old wineskins. Otherwise, the new wine will burst the skins, it will spill, and the skins will be ruined. No, new wine is put into fresh wineskins."

Look at how many times the word *new* appears in those verses. Jesus did not come to be the duct tape patching up our leaky religion. He came to make all things new.

In the Gospels, Jesus came to reset this world. He was not concerned with religious rules or display, but rather with bringing revival and making a way to the Father for all. He shook this world to wake us up and realign our purpose.

And by His Spirit, He still does.

Jeremiah 9 contains a powerful word about divine reset. Verse 23 says, "Thus saith the LORD: The wise should not boast in his wisdom; the strong should not boast in his strength; the wealthy should not boast of his riches. But let him boast of this: that he understands and knows me—that I am the LORD, showing loving-kindness, justice, and righteousness on the earth, for I delight in these things."

Jeremiah is known as the weeping prophet. If you are already depressed, the book of Jeremiah will probably not be your go-to for devotional time. Why did this young prophet weep? Because the people had departed from God and everything was falling to pieces, families were torn to shreds, and the culture was collapsing around him.

Sound familiar?

We want the coronavirus to disappear, for racial harmony to arise, for dignity to reassert itself, for unity to be magnified and manifested. Jeremiah said that first, there must be a resetting of priorities. We must stop defining success by society's standards and replace it with kingdom standards.

Social media has created a culture of boasting, the amplification of personal achievement independent of God, singing hallelujah to yourself, proclaiming that you made it on your own. "Blessed and highly favored" becomes something of a cliché, a sideways brag, looking good on the outside while the spirit slowly dies. Success is not measured by money, power, position, or the amount of education you possess. Arrogance ticks God off, and He will swiftly remind us of our dependency.

The virus doesn't care how much money is in your bank account, whether you have a GED or a PhD or two million followers on the latest platform. Diseases don't care if you've got a Philippians 4:13 bumper sticker on your Lexus and attend the biggest church in town. The virus is an equal-opportunity infector, and it has revealed the limitations of our humanity. It has left us as the Temptations sang—in a ball of confusion.

It's a good thing, then, that Jesus came for the sick and not the healthy. God desires to give us another opportunity to embrace humility, realign culture, and return to Him. As a nation, we are too divided, and we have strayed too far. Politics is not the solution. Social action is not the solution. These are important, but they are not the main thing. The solution is to return our hearts to God and lead by example.

The church needs to wake up and be salt and light to this dying world. This might require that we push out beyond our comfort zones and look for new ways of doing things. Choose a public school to support. Mentor youth from broken homes. Adopt a local police precinct. The church should set the stage by influencing relations between the community and law enforcement, providing counseling and support and inviting both sides in. Isaiah 58:12 calls us to be repairers of the broken walls and a restorer of streets. Build a bridge with someone who is different from you. Then band together and find someone else to help the two of you.

Find where people are struggling, and show up.

The key to reconciliation is service, not seminars. If anyone should be able to move beyond cultural differences and work together, hand in hand, it is God's church. Feed the hungry. Clothe the naked. Care for the sick. Cry with those who mourn. Find where people are struggling, and show up. Service opens the doors to relationship and a faith that can grow organically rather than being forced.

In crisis, there is no division, only need. Now is the time to go beyond the four walls of church. Jesus wants to reset our priorities. When believers are willing to step out and put biblical theology into issues such as injustice, unity, and reconciliation—visibly, not just through words—then we can set a different tone and partner with the Lord to create a divine reset.

NINETEEN

WHAT MATTERS MOST

I have set before you life and death, blessing and curse. Choose life so that you and your descendants may live, love the LORD your God, obey him, and remain faithful to him. For he is your life, and he will prolong your days as you live in the land the LORD swore to give to your ancestors Abraham, Isaac, and Jacob.

—DEUTERONOMY 30:19–20

ANTHONY

Our grandparents taught Mom and Dad to lean toward hope, and in turn, my parents instilled that in us. What can you make from this scenario? How can you look for the good and make a challenging situation work out for your best? It was embedded in me to look at crises as opportunities to do things in a new and different way.

That's how *Divine Disruption* came to be. Our family talked about writing a book together for years, but we were always too busy to get on the same page. Well, the pandemic took care of that. Here we were, all in Dallas, spending more time with each other, talking about the things that matter. But we knew the writing process would be unusual because work, and the way we have conversations, has changed. We've had to collaborate with the book team on Zoom and by email, audio notes, and texts, all flying back and forth.

It makes me think back to that Wednesday-night church service when we were all in shock over Wynter's passing. We got up on the platform in sweatpants and sneakers, no sleep, nothing prepared, just struggling to share the pain that was so heavy in our chests. And somehow the video of that service has been viewed over a million times, more than any other on our church's website. I don't know what that sounds like to you, but it seems the Lord might be trying to tell us something.

> **A lot of things we thought were so important don't matter as much anymore.**

An informal approach was right for that moment, and I believe it was a sign of things to come. People are letting their guard down, going unrehearsed. Less polish, more heart and soul. It doesn't have to be practiced or perfect. A lot of things we thought were so important don't matter as much anymore.

Everything is different now. But Mom and Dad planted that into us from the time we were kids. Different is not always bad. It can be an opportunity for something new. Opportunity is a choice. God partners with us, but faith requires a certain responsibility to accept and make change.

PRISCILLA

The pace of our lives has always been fast. Mom would remind us over and over again, "Slow down. Take time. Stop and smell the roses before they're gone." She could see from the outside looking in that if we weren't mindful of our schedules and commitments, we could easily be overrun by them. Her wise counsel continues to help me make decisions about the pace and priorities in my life. Balance is tough, but it's an ongoing pursuit.

I don't minimize the hardships we've all been through, but they did present an opportunity to be still. Enjoy time with my husband and kids without a 6:00 a.m. cross-country flight hanging over my head. Even in this tragedy, there have been so many moments of tiny grace. Little opportunities to breathe all the way in and all the way out again. I don't want to miss that or take it for granted.

Mom always made time for sunsets.

TONY

The pandemic forced me to reorient my priorities. Not just new programs to implement, but to reconsider what matters most and how I can focus on those things intentionally.

Some of those old things we did out of habit and routine were

> I can't go back to the way things used to be. I don't want to. God has brought me and my family a new normal, and we are pressing on.

undone in an instant. In the light of all this loss, I was reminded that relationships are what matter. Not routines. Family matters. I don't have to fill a sports arena and preach to be content and feel a sense of purpose. Time with my grandkids is just as fulfilling, and even more so. Kids grow up so fast, and once you lose that time, it's gone.

I can't go back to the way things used to be. I don't want to. God has brought me and my family a new normal, and we are pressing on.

JONATHAN

Faith is depending on God when you're living in the unknown, and sometimes the Lord lets us hit rock bottom so we can experience that He *is* the Rock at the bottom. Mom and Dad always told us that your greatest ministry is born from your greatest misery. The most important lessons we learn are in hard times.

PRISCILLA

Life is so short. Eight months after Mommy, my mother-in-law passed away. Another major loss. Another long process of grieving. We didn't have time with Jerry's mom like we did with my mother though. She passed suddenly. I don't want to take any of my loved ones for granted. I want to appreciate every moment, best that I can, and invest in things that give joy, have eternal value, and build a good legacy for generations to come.

ANTHONY

Even right now, in this moment of writing this book, we are all sitting around the dinner table as a family. How rare is that? How much of a blessing is it for all of us to be here together? But if the house suddenly caught fire, we would run and grab those things that matter most: family heirlooms and old photographs.

Well, that's what happened. The world is on fire. The lives we built are going up in smoke. That will rearrange your priorities. And what we did was grab on to each other.

I'm grateful God has blessed our ministries, for big arenas and crowds that are encouraged by what we do, with books and music and sermon series—but that's not what matters most at the end of the day. We have lost so many loved ones. I want to make the best of whatever time we have left together.

JONATHAN

Life is too hard not to play. My wife and I decided to take a vacation with our kids and just go play. It had been six years since we'd experienced snow in Dallas (and by snow, I'm talking about the measly one to two inches that we get excited about every few years). Our kids had been praying for snow, and since their prayers hadn't been answered yet, we planned a winter trip to Colorado.

The kids loved every minute of learning to ski, sledding down hills, and hours of playing in the snow. When you grow up in flat, hot Texas, snowcapped mountains are like a little taste of heaven. God doesn't get mad at His kids for having fun. Jesus walked this earth. He knows how difficult it is.

> The best thing we can do is love God and enjoy this short life with the people we love.

In Ecclesiastes, King Solomon said that we make all these plans and strain and strive and work ourselves to death, and at the end of the day, it's all just smoke in the wind. "Vanity of vanities," he said. The best thing we can do is love God and enjoy this short life with the people we love.

CHRYSTAL

So many of the things we stress about aren't really that important. I think back over all the years, all the questions and concerns I would bring to Mom and Daddy about financial struggles or raising my kids. It all seemed so heavy at the time, but they would keep reassuring me, "Things will work out. It'll be okay. Trust the Lord. Faith will lead you through."

Those problems seem so small now. Most of them did work out as I pressed forward and did the next right thing. Even when life hasn't gone exactly the way I've hoped or planned, God has been faithful to cause things to work together for good. Whether I go left or right, the Lord is with me.

This has been true even when the world shut down and my family walked through the craziest season of our lives. Even as we have lost those closest to us, even as the storms of life rage on and on. It hurts and it's hard, but the Lord has been with us. We are going to be okay.

No matter what you are going through, I believe this for you too. Hold tight to God.

You are going to be okay.

TWENTY ———

LEGACY LIVES ON

See, I am doing a new thing!
Now it springs up; do you not perceive it?
I am making a way in the wilderness
and streams in the wasteland.

ISAIAH 43:19 NIV

ANTHONY

I'm standing at the stove in my mother's kitchen, making her famous pancakes. I wonder how many stacks of pancakes Mom made standing in this very same spot. I wonder how many meals she cooked here over forty years. How many hungry people did she feed? Hundreds? Thousands? At least thousands. My mother had a servant's heart.

Times are still kind of stressful. Just as a rare Dallas blizzard nearly destroyed the ministry offices, Dad caught COVID. Mom's pancakes are his favorite, so I'm making up a batch for him. Thank God, he's been mostly asymptomatic so far. He even preached Sunday morning, broadcasting the message from home. Mom was fiercely protective of Dad, so I want to help take care of him as best I can. "Keep the ministry going," she told us.

Eggs, milk, flour. A few of her secret ingredients here and there. Even the sound of a fork stirring a ceramic bowl reminds me so much of my mom. We made it through the anniversary of her passing, and all I can really say is it was bittersweet, difficult in ways I can't even begin to explain. But sweet, too, because we realized what a wonderful legacy she left for us to share. I don't know why we have to lose something to fully appreciate its significance. But that's how it seems to work down here.

> I don't know why we have to lose something to fully appreciate its significance. But that's how it seems to work down here.

The first Christmas without your loved one is tough. My mother loved the holidays and always made it an extra-special time. Growing up in Guyana, Mom's family didn't really celebrate Christmas. Their tradition was to celebrate on New Year's Day. After my parents married, Mom made up for lost time.

She would prepare the biggest, most elaborate Christmas feast you have ever laid your eyes on. All by herself! Huge meals are the South American way, and Mom married that notion to Texas-sized thinking. How did she cook so many dishes and serve them while they were still hot? I'm shocked the table didn't collapse under the weight of all that food. We are still amazed at how she managed to get so much done.

When Mom's health began to decline, Priscilla made videos of her walking through the preparation of her signature dishes. Mom put on a cooking class for us so we could keep her tradition going strong.

Christmas 2020 came around. I was fighting back anxiety, feeling down. My parents moved into this house when I was three years old. Even with four rambunctious kids, Mom and Dad never built on to our home, but Christmas seemed to get bigger every year.

The Temptations' *Christmas Card* album was my father's favorite, and I can still hear their version of "Silent Night" ringing through the house. Mom kept her holiday favorites on repeat too: Kenny G., Michael Bublé, Gladys Knight. Dad would be dancing around the living room while Mom cooked and baked up an endless display of treats in the kitchen. At night, our neighborhood was bumper-to-bumper traffic, cars crawling down our street so people could see the houses in our neighborhood lit up in all their Christmas glory.

Mom made our home look like Santa and his elves had moved the North Pole to south Dallas. Wreaths and bows and candles, trees in every room, a thousand twinkling tiny lights. Presents stacked everywhere, cookies laid out on the table Christmas Eve. My father would eat them all and there would be crumbs in his mustache. Like, hold up, Dad! Did you eat Santa's cookies?

Fast-forward to Christmas 2020. I stood in front of our house for a long time, thinking about all the memories we shared, wondering what the future might hold without Mom. Yeah, I'm the sensitive kid. I have to think about things.

Finally, I walked inside. I could hear the rattle and hiss of the pressure cooker making rice, the rich, smoky scent of fresh paprika and cayenne drifting down the hall. Pepper pot, cook-up rice and peas—that's what Christmas at home smells like to me, and for just one moment, it felt like Mom was still here.

I rounded the corner into the kitchen. My sisters were watching the video of Mom's cooking class, laughing, bustling around with cabinet doors open, clanging pans, spinning the spice rack looking for Scotch bonnet. I couldn't help but get choked up. With Mom's help, Chrystal and Priscilla were making our big family Christmas come together again.

And not just the food. There were decorations everywhere: Jesus and Christmas trees, nativity scenes, burning candles, nonstop carols. And then I realized something. Mom *is* here. She's here through Priscilla, through Chrystal, through Jonathan, and through me. Here through the grandkids and great-grandchildren as they run around the house she loved so.

> **As a kid, you take so much for granted. Then you grow up and realize what a gift you have been given and what a privilege it is to carry those traditions forward.**

As a kid, you take so much for granted. Then you grow up and realize what a gift you have been given and what a privilege it is to carry those traditions forward. The best thing you can leave behind is a good legacy. In that sense, Mommy will never leave. We will always have a part of her here with us.

"Kanika and I were driving over," Jonathan told me on Christmas morning, "and I looked at her and it hit me—she is living the life my mother lived. Minister's wife, five kids. Dad showed us through example how to be an attentive father and husband, but I want to fine-tune it, take it a step higher, make sure she is never overlooked or unappreciated. That's what Mom and Daddy would want."

Jonathan is in a position to take over some things at the church now. Oh, don't worry. Daddy isn't going anywhere anytime soon. As long as he has breath, he will serve God's people and preach the Word. But Jonathan is in place to follow in his footsteps, and when that time comes, he will be ready.

I'm still splitting my time between Dallas and Los Angeles. Some say Texas *is* the new California. I guess we'll see. I think about my mother's dedication to excellence, seeing the evidence of it all around. I want to be faithful and diligent with family and friends, in work, play, and serving God. Legacy inspires legacy. I want to leave a good mark too.

I think about all the loved ones we have lost over the last few years. The Bible says they will not return to us, but we shall join them. On that day it will be all sweet and no bitter, all peace and joy, no more loss or grief or pain. Because of the hope we have in Christ, we will see

Mommy again. That takes away a bit of death's sting. Until then, we will carry the mantle, and we will carry on.

Thank you for taking this journey with us, for walking through the adventures of our first family book. God has reminded us that life is so futile and fleeting. We are only passing through.

There is a time for everything. To laugh and to cry. To grieve and to dance. A time to be silent and another to speak. Not just for the Evans, Hurst, and Shirer families, but for all of God's family. Even when life breaks our hearts, we can still hold on. To faith. To love. To promises. To hope. And to each other.

All of us together, trusting God.

ACKNOWLEDGMENTS

The Evans, Hurst, and Shirer families would like to thank W Publishing for taking on such a personal project. Special thanks to Debbie Wickwire, Jamie Blaine, Ashley Irons, Dawn Hollomon, Tracy Alderson, and Summer Pennino for their willingness to walk step-by-step with us through this process and for their incomparable diligence.

To all of the readers who have taken this personal journey with us—we are thankful for you and what you collectively mean to our family. You have helped us honor our mom's wishes, and for that we are eternally grateful.

ABOUT THE AUTHORS

Dr. Tony Evans is a pastor, bestselling author, and frequent speaker at Bible conferences and seminars across the nation. He has served as senior pastor of Oak Cliff Bible Fellowship for more than forty years, witnessing its growth from ten people in 1976 to now over ten thousand congregants with one hundred-plus ministries. Dr. Evans is founder of The Urban Alternative, a Christian Bible-teaching and resource ministry. His radio broadcast, *The Alternative with Tony Evans*, can be heard on over 1,400 radio outlets daily and in more than 130 countries. Dr. Evans was married to Lois, his wife and ministry partner, for nearly fifty years. They have four children, thirteen grandchildren, and three great-grandchildren.

Chrystal Evans Hurst is an energetic, fun-loving "girl next door" who loves to encourage other women in fulfilling their full potential in Christ. Chrystal is a gifted writer, speaker, worship leader, and most importantly, the COO of the Hurst household. Chrystal is a dedicated wife to her husband, Jessie, and homeschooling mother of five: Kariss, Jessica, Jesse III, Kanaan, and Joel. Chrystal and her family reside in a small town just outside of Dallas, Texas.

Priscilla Shirer is a wife and a mom first, but put a Bible in her hand and a message in her heart and you'll see why thousands meet God in powerful, personal ways at her conferences and through her Bible studies. For the past twenty years Priscilla has been in full-time ministry to women. She and her husband, Jerry, founded Going Beyond Ministries, and they count it as their privilege to serve believers across the spectrum of the body of Christ. Priscilla is passionate about ministry but prioritizes her calling as wife and mother above all. Between writing and studying, she spends her days cleaning up after (and trying to satisfy the appetites of) three rapidly growing sons: Jackson, Jerry Jr., and Jude.

Anthony Evans has voiced the gospel for more than a decade with such a melodic, thought-provoking style that he has emerged as one of Christian music's premier male vocalists, songwriters, and worship leaders. His time in Los Angeles with NBC's hit show *The Voice* led him to think more progressively about his music without compromising his faith and message. With nine solo projects and multiple music videos, Anthony has set the tone by using his skill-set and desire for excellence both inside the church and beyond.

Jonathan Evans, a mentor, author, speaker, and former NFL fullback, seeks to impact today's athletes, men, and young adults by equipping and encouraging them in their faith. Jonathan serves with his pastor, friend, and father, Dr. Tony Evans, in both the local church and national ministry. Jonathan is a graduate of Dallas Theological Seminary with a master's degree in Christian leadership. He serves as the chaplain of the Dallas Cowboys and co-chaplain of the Dallas Mavericks. Jonathan and his wife, Kanika, are the proud parents of Kelsey, Jonathan II, Kamden, Kylar, and Jade Wynter. They reside in Dallas, Texas.

Dr. Lois Evans served as first lady of Oak Cliff Bible Fellowship for over four decades, was senior vice president of The Urban Alternative, and is the founder of Pastors' Wives Ministry. An accomplished pianist, singer, speaker, and author, she was the full expression of a Proverbs 31 woman, living a life of integrity, character, and excellence, loving on friends and family, leaving her footprints everywhere she went. Lois was married for nearly fifty years to her favorite pastor and teacher and best friend. They never stopped dating, working side by side, serving God, and taking lots of selfies together while having fun.

She is home now with Jesus, enjoying the never-ending sunrise.

KINGDOM
LEGACY

EVANS · HURST · SHIRER

KingdomLegacy.com

 kingdomlegacylive

DR. TONY
EVANS

TonyEvans.org

 drtonyevans

drtonyevans

drtonyevans

drtonyevans

CHRYSTAL EVANS
─ H U R S T ─

ChrystalEvansHurst.com

ChrystalHurst

chrystalhurst

ChrystalHurst

ChrystalHurst

PRISCILLA
—— SHIRER ——

GoingBeyond.com

GoingBeyondMinistries

priscillashirer

PriscillaShirer

GoingBeyondMinistries

ANTHONY
EVANS

Anthony-Evans.com

 anthonyevansmusic

anthonyevansjr

AnthonyEvansJr

anthonyevansofficial

JONATHAN
EVANS

JonathanBlakeEvans.com

 jonathanblakeevans

jonathanblakeevans

EvansLegacy

DR. TONY EVANS

CELEBRATING

40 Years of Faithfulness in Ministry

Blessed are those who fear the Lord and walk in His ways.

Psalm 128